The Word in the World

THE SOCIETY OF BIBLICAL LITERATURE
MONOGRAPH SERIES

E.F. Campbell, Editor
Jouette M. Bassler, Associate Editor

Number 45
THE WORD IN THE WORLD
The Cosmological Tale in the Fourth Gospel

by
Adele Reinhartz

Adele Reinhartz

THE WORD IN THE WORLD
The Cosmological Tale
in the Fourth Gospel

Scholars Press
Atlanta, Georgia

THE WORD IN THE WORLD

by
Adele Reinhartz

The Greek font used to print this work is available
from Linguist's Software, Inc., PO Box 580,
Edmonds, WA 98020-0580 tel (206)775-1130.

Library of Congress Cataloging in Publication Data
Reinhartz, Adele, 1953-
    The word in the world: the cosmological tale in the fourth Gospel
/ Adele Reinhartz.
        p. cm. — (Monograph series / the Society of Biblical
Literature; no. 45)
    Includes bibliographical references and indexes.
    ISBN 1-55540-798-6 (cloth: alk. paper). — ISBN 1-55540-799-4
(pbk.: alk. paper)
    1. Bible. N.T. John—Criticism, interpretation, etc. 2. Bible.
N.T. John —Theology. I. Title. II. Series: Monograph series
(Society of Biblical Literature); no. 45.
BS2615.2.R384   1992
226.5'06—dc20   92-38139
                                                       CIP

Printed in the United States of America
on acid-free paper

TABLE OF CONTENTS

Contents

ABBREVIATIONS

AB   R. E. Brown. *The Gospel According to John*. The Anchor Bible, 29–
            29A. New York: Doubleday, 1966–70.

Culpepper   R. Alan Culpepper. *Anatomy of the Fourth Gospel*. Philadelphia:
            Fortress, 1983.

Ashton   John Ashton, ed. *The Interpretation of John*. Issues in Religion and
            Theology 9. Philadelphia: Fortress, 1986.

Bultmann   Rudolf Bultmann. *The Gospel of John*. Philadelphia: Westminster,
            1971.

Dodd   C. H. Dodd. *The Interpretation of the Fourth Gospel*. Cambridge:
            Cambridge University, 1953.

Godet   F. Godet. *Commentary on the Gospel of St. John*, vol. 2. 3rd ed.
            Edinburgh: T. and T. Clark, 1892.

Quasten   John Quasten. "The Parable of the Good Shepherd: Jn.10:1–21."
            CBQ 10 (1948): 1–12, 151–69.

Schnack.   Rudolf Schnackenburg. *The Gospel According to John*, 3 vols. New
            York: Crossroad, 1980–82.

Simonis   A. J. Simonis. *Die Hirtenrede im Johannes-evangelium*. Rom:
            Päpstliches Bibelsinstitut, 1967.

Other abbreviations used in this volume can be found in the *Journal of Biblical
Literature* 107 (1988) 579–96.

ACKNOWLEDGEMENTS

The final form and substance of the present study bear little relationship to the observations and ideas with which I began my investigation. The point which I initially intended to investigate was whether the gatekeeper in John 10:3 was an allusion to the mythical keeper of the gates of Hades. What began as a limited history-of-religions quest (now relegated to the appendix of this book) gradually took on a life of its own as an exploration of the different levels, or tales, within the Johannine narrative as a whole.

Of the many people—colleagues, students, friends, family—whose work, patient attention, and comments contributed to this metamorphosis, I wish to single out a few for special mention: Robert Kysar and R. Alan Culpepper, whose thoughtful comments on the manuscript provided both encouragement and substantive suggestions for furthering my reflections on the cosmological tale in the Fourth Gospel; Jouette M. Bassler, New Testament editor, SBL Monograph Series, whose courteous and efficient assistance was much appreciated; Norma Graham-Heggie, who helped in the initial gathering of secondary source material on John 10; my colleagues Stephen Westerholm and Gérard Vallée, who read the manuscript in its early stages. I wish also to acknowledge gratefully the assistance of Social Sciences and Humanities Research Council of Canada, which provided seed-funds in the early stages of the research, as well as McMaster University, which helped in the preparation of the final manuscript through a university research grant.

Finally, I thank my family: my parents, for their unwavering support of my endeavors; my children, for their hugs and antics, which kept me anchored and smiling in the here and now; and, above all, my spouse, Barry Walfish, for his encouragement, his editorial skills, his expertise in the kitchen and the nursery, and his love. It is to him that I dedicate this book.

INTRODUCTION

New Testament exegetes, like scholars in many other fields, are increasingly concerned with the relationship between the text and the reader. In attempting to describe and account for that relationship, they have been turning to the work of reader-response critics such as Stanley Fish and Wolfgang Iser.[1] Although the assumptions and insights of reader-response criticism have been applied to most if not all of the New Testament, this approach has been most influential in the study of the gospel narratives.[2] The present study is intended as a contribution to the ongoing conversation about readers and readings of the Gospel of John. Its specific focus will be the implied reader's construction and utilization of the gospel's story in reading and making sense of the Fourth Gospel as a whole.

The Fourth Gospel has been and continues to be subject to a multiplicity of readings. The vigorous debates over Johannine eschatology, christology, symbolic language, and meaning testify to the openness of this text to multivalent readings and attempts at consistency-building. Behind many of these attempts, however, lie three related, though often unarticulated, assumptions. First, the text is a narrative. Second, this narrative is, to borrow a narratological term from Gérard Genette, a "signifier."[3] Like other narrative texts, this signifier tells a story.[4] This story may be termed the "signified" or the narrative content of the narrative text.[5] Finally, the "signified" or story of the Johannine narrative has

---

[1] There has been some debate, however, about whether what New Testament scholars call reader-response criticism is in fact that. See Stanley E. Porter, "Why Hasn't Reader-Response Criticism Caught on in New Testament Studies?" *Journal of Literature and Theology* 4 (1990) 278–92. For a different analysis of the impact of reader-response criticism, see Stephen D. Moore, *Literary Criticism and the Gospels: The Theoretical Challenge* (New Haven: Yale University Press, 1989).

[2] See, for example, Jeffrey Lloyd Staley, *The Print's First Kiss: A Rhetorical Investigation of the Implied Reader in the Fourth Gospel* (SBLDS 82; Atlanta: Scholars Press, 1988), and the essays in *Reader Perspectives on the New Testament*, ed. Edgar V. McKnight, *Semeia* 48 (1989).

[3] Gérard Genette, *Narrative Discourse: An Essay in Method* (Ithaca: Cornell University Press, 1980) 27.

[4] That the gospels are first and foremost stories is emphasized by Frank Kermode, who argues against foregrounding of the source-critical enterprise by suggesting that "the critic who attends to the story rather than to some lost narrative it replaced perhaps is attending to the first requirement of the Gospels." See Kermode, "John," *The Literary Guide to the Bible* (ed. Robert Alter and Frank Kermode; Cambridge: Harvard University Press, 1987) 441–42.

[5] Genette, *Narrative Discourse*, 27. One could also use Chatman's distinction between discourse (the narrative) and story, although this terminology would be confusing in the

a plot, that is, a sequence of actions "rendered" toward achieving particular emotional and artistic effects."[6] Although the plot of the Fourth Gospel's story of Jesus can be described and charted in many different ways,[7] its central element is the conflict between hero—Jesus—and villain—Jesus' opponents—over Jesus' identity, a conflict which reaches its climax and resolution in the Passion. The death of Jesus expresses the antagonists' ultimate rejection of his claims, and hence the failure of Jesus' attempts to persuade them otherwise. Jesus' death evokes sorrow in his followers (20:1) and also, potentially, in the readers, until it is dramatically reversed by his resurrection appearances in chapter 20. The markers within the text that signal this plot are the characters named and described within the gospel and the actions attributed to them, as well as geographical and temporal details that root the plot in space and time.

This narrative content, or story, may be said to constitute a historical tale, for two reasons. First, its setting—early first-century C.E. Palestine—is that of the historical Jesus. Second, though episodic (20:30) and dramatic, it is meant to be read as a "true" account of events which really happened. This is emphasized by the narrator, who in 21:24 expresses his[8] concern that the readers consider as true the testimony of "the disciple who is testifying to these things and has written them...."[9] The historical tale is accessible to all readers of the Fourth Gospel and might be described as the primary "signified" or content towards which the gospel as signifier is generally thought to point.

But even a first reading of this gospel raises the suspicion that it does more than tell a historical tale. For example, there are details which, though clearly

---

context of Johannine scholarship, for which the term "discourse" signifies Jesus' lengthy speeches, as in the "Bread of Life" discourse (John 6) and the Farewell Discourses (John 13–17). See Seymour Chatman, *Story and Discourse: Narrative Structure in Fiction and Film* (Ithaca: Cornell University Press, 1978). For a strong challenge to Chatman's "two-storey model," see Moore, *Literary Criticism*, 43–68.

[6] M. H. Abrams, *A Glossary of Literary Terms* (3rd ed.; New York: Holt, Rinehart and Winston, 1971) 127. For a list of other definitions, see Culpepper, 79–80.

[7] For a brief survey of of the ways in which the plot or structure has been described, see Fernando F. Segovia, "The Journey(s) of the Word of God: A Reading of the Plot of the Fourth Gospel," *The Fourth Gospel From a Literary Perspective*, ed. R. Alan Culpepper and Fernando F. Segovia, *Semeia* 53 (1991) 26–31.

[8] Although we do not know the identity of the "real" author, the implied author of the gospel is the Beloved Disciple, hence the use of the masculine pronoun. This does not necessarily mean that the "real" author was male, but in my view this is likely, despite the fact that, as scholars have noted, the Fourth Gospel places stories about women at crucial points in the narrative. See Elisabeth Schüssler Fiorenza, *In Memory of Her* (New York: Crossroad, 1986) 326, and AB 1.xcii–xcviii.

[9] Cf. also 19:35. All quotations are from the New Revised Standard Version (1989), unless otherwise noted.

part of the historical tale told by the gospel, may seem out of context in the life of the historical Jesus himself. These include references to the exclusion of Jesus' followers from the synagogue (9:22; 16:2), an event which is generally dated to the latter part of the first century, at least fifty years after the crucifixion event. Raymond E. Brown[10] and J. Louis Martyn,[11] among others, drew on such details and other features of the gospel to read a second story in the Johannine narrative. This is the story of the Johannine community at the end of the first century C.E. in the Greek Diaspora.[12] This story too has a plot, which revolves around the conflict between the Johannine community and the synagogue in its city over issues of belief and unbelief. Because its setting is the life of the Johannine church, this story may be called an ecclesiological tale.

The historical tale is perceived by means of a realistic reading of the gospel narrative, in which, for example, the signifier "Jesus" in the narrative is taken to signify the character Jesus in the story, the "disciples" in the narrative signify Jesus' disciples in the story, and so on. In contrast, the ecclesiological tale is perceived by means of what may be termed a representational reading of the narrative text. For example, the signifier "Jesus" in the narrative is taken to represent the Christian preacher in the ecclesiological tale; the "disciples" are thought to represent the post–Easter Johannine community; the "Jews" represent the late first-century synagogue in conflict with the church.[13]

In fact, it may be suggested that for readers interested in the gospel for what it reveals about the Johannine community, the historical tale itself becomes a signifier, with the ecclesiological tale as its narrative content. The encounter between Jesus and the Samaritans, signified by the narrative in John 4, for example, in turn signifies the acceptance of Samaritan believers into the Johannine community.[14] The experience of Jesus and his followers in the historical tale signifies the experience of the community. Hence the conflict between Jesus and the Jews in John 9 can be read as a paradigm for the strained relations between Johannine Christians and their Jewish antagonists after the expulsion of Jewish Christians from the synagogue.[15] The words of the Johannine

---

[10] Raymond E. Brown, *The Community of the Beloved Disciple* (New York: Paulist, 1979).

[11] J. Louis Martyn, *History and Theology in the Fourth Gospel* (2d ed.; Nashville: Abingdon, 1979). For a recent discussion and summary of the state of the question, see John Ashton, *Understanding the Fourth Gospel* (Oxford: Clarendon, 1991) 166–74.

[12] For a discussion of provenance, see AB 1.ciii–civ.

[13] This is Martyn's reading of John 9. See Martyn, *History*, 37–62.

[14] Brown, *Community*, 36–40.

[15] Martyn, *History*, 29–30, 38–62, 156–7; Brown, *Community*, 22; compare Reuven Kimelman, "*Birkat Ha-Minim* and the Lack of Evidence for an Anti-Christian Jewish Prayer in Late Antiquity," *Jewish and Christian Self-Definition* (ed. E. P. Sanders; Philadelphia: Fortress, 1981) 2.226–55, 391–403.

Jesus, while directed to a specific audience within the narrative, are taken to address the situation of the Johannine community.[16] In this way, says Martyn, "The text is also a witness to Jesus' powerful presence in actual events experienced by the Johannine church."[17] If the historical tale is the primary tale told by the narrative text, the ecclesiological tale may be labeled the sub-tale which moves beneath its surface.

Rich as these two tales are, however, they do not exhaust the levels of the narrative content of the Fourth Gospel. Rather, specific hints in the gospel intimate that its story goes well beyond the temporal and geographical boundaries of the historical and ecclesiological tales. These hints appear as early as 1:1, those famous words with which our gospel begins: "In the beginning was the Word, and the Word was with God, and the Word was God." This passage, and many others like it, point to the presence of yet another story in this gospel, with its own set of dramatis personae and its particular emotional impact upon the reader. This tale has the cosmos as its setting and eternity as its time frame. Its hero is the pre-existent Word who becomes flesh, having been sent by God his Father into the world to bring salvation. The villain is the "ruler of this world" (14:30), "the evil one" (17:15), Satan (13:27), or the devil (8:44; 13:2).[18] As in the historical tale, the struggle between hero and villain reaches its climax in the Passion narrative. The death of Jesus on the cross marks not his failure but his success: it signifies the successful completion of his mission, the "casting out" of the ruler of this world (12:31), and the beginning of the hero's return to his Father from whom he had come forth. The appropriate emotional response to this death is not sorrow but joy (16:20). Furthermore, Jesus' death and departure from the world is not a rupture in the relationship between Jesus and his followers, but rather a new phase, marked by the presence of the paraclete, whom Jesus will send after his departure (16:7).

Because of its cosmic setting, this sequence of events may be said to constitute a cosmological tale, in no sense less "true" than the historical and ecclesiological tales. The cosmological tale intersects and parallels the historical

---

16 The two stories are linked not only through parallelism but also through the signifier "Beloved Disciple." This signifier in the narrative text points to Jesus' favorite disciple in the historical tale, the one who reclined next to him at the last supper (13:23, 25) and to whom Jesus gave over the care of his mother (19:27). The analysis of Brown (*Community*, 31–34, 89) suggests that the "Beloved Disciple," unlike other signifiers in the Fourth Gospel, is to be understood as the same signified within the ecclesiological tale as within the historical tale. That is, the same person who was Jesus' favored disciple within the historical tale was the founder or leader of the Johannine community.

17 Martyn, *History*, 30.

18 Cf. C. J. Coetzee, "Christ and the Prince of this World in the Gospel and the Epistles of St. John," *Neot* 2 (1968) 104–21.

and ecclesiological tales at many points. Indeed, it may be said that the cosmological tale provides the narrative framework into which the other tales are set. The two- to three-year time span of Jesus' earthly mission—the "story time" of the historical tale—and the period of the Johannine church—the "story-time" of the ecclesiological tale—are placed in the continuum of the Word's pre-existence with God and the eventual return of the Word and his disciples to God's realm, that is, the "story time" of the cosmological tale.[19] The geographical settings of the historical and ecclesiological tales, namely, Palestine (including Judea, Samaria and Galilee) and the Diaspora respectively, have their place in the cosmos, the geographical setting of the cosmological tale. Furthermore, the three tales intersect at many different points. To give just one example, the Jewish villains of the historical tale are spiritual kin not only to the messengers who informed the Jewish community in John's city of the Jamnian decision to exclude Christians from the synagogue, or to the members of the local Gerousia who enforced this decision,[20] but also to the diabolical villain of the cosmological tale (cf. 8:44).[21]

These observations suggest that the cosmological tale is the meta-tale, which provides the overarching temporal, geographical, theological, and narrative framework for the other two tales. The cosmological tale shares certain features of the other two tales. Like the historical tale, it reads the gospel narrative realistically. The "Jesus" of the narrative does not signify or represent someone other than the Jesus of the historical tale. Rather, the Jesus of the historical tale is seen to be the very Word of the cosmological tale. The physical and temporal setting of the historical tale is not representative of another place and time, as in an ecclesiological reading of the gospel, but rather is situated in the larger context of the cosmos, according to the cosmological tale. Like the ecclesiological tale, however, the cosmological tale constitutes an implicit commentary on the historical tale; as such, it adds depth and texture to the gospel narrative and richness to the reading experience.

That there is a narrative schema with cosmic dimensions operative in the Fourth Gospel has not gone completely unnoticed by Johannine scholars. Indeed, this point has been developed in detail by Rudolf Bultmann, who saw its origins in a Gnostic myth of the Redeemer.[22] But whereas Bultmann, his

---

[19] For a definition and discussion of "story-time", see Genette, *Narrative Discourse*, 33–35; Culpepper, 53–75.

[20] This is according to Martyn, *History*, 61.

[21] This is seen also in 13:27, in which Judas, the agent of Jesus' betrayal in the historical tale, is directly associated with Satan, who entered into him.

[22] See Rudolf Bultmann, *Theology of the New Testament* (New York: Charles Scribner's Sons, 1955), Vol. 2, Part III; also his commentary, passim. The relationship between cosmology and

supporters, and his detractors argued about the implications of this myth for historical and source criticism of the Fourth Gospel,[23] only recently have scholars begun to pay attention to its role in the narrative and its impact on the reader. Robert Kysar, for example, comments that John's story of Jesus "is indeed a story of a human on the plane of history; but it is at the same time the story of one who comes from beyond the world and from the beginning of all existence."[24] Fernando Segovia has argued that the "mythological, cosmic journey" of the Word of God provides a framework for the other journeys which structure the plot of this gospel.[25] These works and others which touch on aspects of the cosmological tale[26] suggest the need for a more comprehensive study of the cosmological tale, its place and function in the gospel narrative, and its utilization by the implied reader constructing a coherent reading of the gospel as a whole. It is to this need that the present study is addressed.

Before commencing, however, it will be useful to define the key terms, assumptions, and aims which will inform our study. We shall assume the objective existence of a real reader—a flesh and blood person engaged in the act of reading—and a real text, namely the Fourth Gospel, as found in the critical edition of Nestle-Aland.[27] Furthermore, we shall consider this gospel to be a work of fiction, a "self-consciously crafted narrative...resulting from literary imagination."[28] Although the possibility that the Fourth Gospel may contain historical data should not be dismissed, this issue is not germane to the present

---

apocalyptic is discussed by Barnabas Lindars, "The Apocalyptic Myth and the Death of Christ," *BJRL* 57 (1974–5) 366–87. Although Lindars focuses primarily on the Synoptic gospels, many of his comments are applicable to the Fourth Gospel as well.

[23] See Schnack. 1.543–57.

[24] Robert Kysar, *John's Story of Jesus* (Philadelphia: Fortress, 1984) 18.

[25] Segovia, "Journey," 23–54.

[26] See, for example, Godfrey C. Nicholson, *Death as Departure* (SBLDS 63; Chico, Calif.: Scholars Press, 1983); Karl Martin Fischer, "Der johanneische Christus und der gnostische Erlöser," *Gnosis und Neues Testament* (ed. Karl-Wolfgang Troeger; Berlin: Gerd Mohn, 1973) 235–266; Wayne A. Meeks "The Man from Heaven in Johannine Sectarianism," *JBL* 91 (1972) 44–72 (reprinted in Ashton, 141–73); M. de Jonge, *Jesus: Stranger from Heaven and Son of God* (SBLSBS 11; Missoula, Mont.: Scholars Press, 1977); D. Bruce Woll, *Johannine Christianity in Conflict* (SBLDS 60; Chico, Calif.: Scholars Press, 1981).

[27] *Novum Testamentum Graece* (26th ed.; Stuttgart: Deutsche Bibelstiftung, 1979).

[28] These words, which Mary Ann Tolbert has applied to the Gospel of Mark, apply equally well to the Fourth Gospel and, no doubt, to the First and Third Gospels as well. See Tolbert, *Sowing the Gospel: Mark's World in Literary-Historical Perspective* (Minneapolis: Fortress, 1989) 30. For more detailed discussion on scripture as fiction, see Robert Alter, *The Art of Biblical Narrative* (New York: Basic, 1981) 24–27.

study. Finally, taking our cue from Seymour Chatman,[29] we shall assume that this text contains three literary constructs accessible to the real reader.

The first is the implied author. The implied author is the image of the author which readers construct as they read the gospel and to whom they attribute the literary strategies of the narrative. In the gospels, the voice of the implied author is that of the narrator who tells the story and speaks to the reader.[30] The attribution of the gospels to the four evangelists, which usually heads any version or translation of the gospel texts which readers are likely to read, also implies an identification of the narrators as the evangelists.[31] Hence the terms evangelist, narrator, and implied author can all be used to refer to aspects of the image of the author to whom the reader attributes the narrative elements and techniques of the text.[32]

The second is the narrative content or story. As a narrative text, the Fourth Gospel tells its story by means of its narration of particular events that follow one another in a particular sequence. The story has an independent existence apart from the narrative only in the mind of the reader, and may be constructed by different real readers in different ways.[33]

The third is the implied reader. Like the implied author and the story, the implied reader exists only in the mind of the real reader and, in the case of the Fourth Gospel, may be identified with, or identical to, the narratees, the party to whom the narrator is addressing his or her words.[34] The implied readers may be reconstructed from the text as those who are capable of understanding the text, its language, its devices, and its message. Hence the implied reader may be defined as the image of the intended reader which a real reader constructs in reading the text.[35]

---

[29] Chatman, *Story and Discourse*, 146–51.

[30] Culpepper, 16.

[31] See Culpepper (213), who at times uses the terms narrator and evangelist interchangeably. The identification of the narrator with the evangelist is especially clear in the Gospel of Luke, in which the narrator provides a rationale in the first person for the writing of his narrative (Luke 1:1–4).

[32] In using the term "evangelist" in this sense, however, it is important to keep in mind that the reference is not to the evangelist as a historical person but to the image of the evangelist that the reader would construct through a reading of the gospel narrative. For discussion of the issue of authorship, see AB 1.lxxxvii–ciii. For detailed discussion of the term "implied author," cf. Culpepper, 15–16.

[33] See Wolfgang Iser, *The Implied Reader* (Baltimore: The Johns Hopkins University Press, 1974) 279.

[34] Culpepper, 208. Note, however, that the identity of the implied reader and narratee is not to be assumed in the case of other texts, such as the Gospel of Luke, in which the narratee is Theophilus, but the implied reader is likely not a single individual but rather a community.

[35] For an introduction to the multiplicity of readers, see Gerald Prince, "Introduction to the Study of the Narratee," *Reader-Response Criticism: From Formalism to Post-structuralism* (ed.

The present study will therefore examine the ways in which one construct of the Fourth Gospel, namely, the implied reader, would derive a second construct, the story or stories embodied in the Johannine narrative, in order to discern the intentions of the third construct, the implied author. Its focus will therefore be on the activity of the implied reader. But who is this implied reader and what does he/she do?

Many scholars have tried, whether "explicitly or implicitly, to identify the implied readers of the Fourth Gospel in their attempts to label the original real readers whom the real author meant to address in writing this gospel.[36] Such attempts focus on what, according to the gospel, the readers are expected and not expected to know, and examine assumptions that are apparently held in common by implied author and implied reader.[37]

One key to the identity of the implied reader is 20:30–31:

> Now Jesus did many other signs in the presence of the disciples, which are not written in this book. But these are written so that you may come to believe [πιστευσῆτε] [or: may continue to believe— πιστεύητε] that Jesus is the Messiah [Christ], the Son of God, and that through believing you may have life in his name.

The textual variant in 20:31 casts some doubt as to whether the addressees are already Christians whom the implied author wishes to edify and strengthen in their faith, or non-Christians whom the implied author aims to persuade. Many scholars argue, however, that in the context of the gospel as a whole, it is the former who are the primary addressees of this gospel.[38] Furthermore, it would

---

Jane P. Tompkins; Baltimore: Johns Hopkins, 1980) 7–25. Prince uses the term "virtual reader" for Iser's implied reader. For a discussion of "gaps," see Iser, *Implied Reader*, 274–80.

[36] An identification of the real "original" reader and the implied reader is assumed by many studies of the addressee and purpose of the gospel. For summaries of the various positions, see Culpepper, 211, and Robert Kysar, *The Fourth Evangelist and his Gospel* (Minneapolis: Augsburg, 1975) 147–65.

[37] Culpepper, 212.

[38] The major manuscripts supporting the present subjunctive are Bezae, Alexandrinus and those of the Byzantine tradition. The aorist subjunctive is supported by Vaticanus, Sinaiticus, and possibly also P66. This reading is followed in Nestle's critical edition. Harald Riesenfeld ("Zu den johanneischen ἵνα-Sätzen," *ST* 19 [1965] 220) suggests that the normal usage of the ἵνα clause is the present subjunctive, a conclusion which would tend to support the theory that the Gospel is directed towards Christians. It must be pointed out, however, that theories of purpose cannot be hung on this point alone, both because the gospel is not consistent in its use of tenses, and also because the aorist subjunctive does not necessarily have to have a future connotation. See Rudolf Schnackenburg, "Die Messiasfrage im Johannesevangelium,"

seem that these addressees were not themselves eye-witnesses to the life of the historical Jesus. Rather, they formed part of a community, probably the community of the evangelist himself, which belonged to the era after the death and resurrection of Christ.[39]

This conclusion can be supported from evidence throughout the Fourth Gospel narrative.[40] It is important to note, however, that the gospel in general, and 20:30–31 in particular, do not explicitly limit their intended audience to a specific community. Rather, they suggest an open definition of the implied readers as those who see themselves as being personally addressed by the verbs in 20:30–31 which are in the second person plural: "you may believe" [$\pi\iota\sigma\tau\epsilon\acute{u}\eta\tau\epsilon$], "you may have life" [$\zeta\omega\grave{\eta}\nu$ $\acute{\epsilon}\chi\eta\tau\epsilon$] "in his name." Such a general definition creates an opening for the real reader to identify with the implied reader. That is, any reader who is open to the message of the gospel and takes seriously the implied author's statement of purpose in 20:30–31 may in fact see himself or herself as being directly addressed by the gospel narrative as well as challenged by its theological perspective.[41] Hence the particular narrative techniques and elements of the text, including the multi-layered narrative itself, will affect not only the implied readers but all of the real readers who identify with them.

In addition to defining who "readers" are, reader-response critics attempt to describe what readers do, that is, the moves the readers make in constructing meaning from, or finding meaning in, the text.[42] Perhaps the most fundamental of these is the observation that the reader will strive to come up with a harmonious or coherent interpretation or reading of the text.[43] As Wolfgang Iser notes, the reader is engaged in

---

Neutestamentliche Aufsätze: Festschrift für Josef Schmid (ed. Josef Blinzler; Regensburg: Pustet, 1963) 257; AB 2.1056.

[39] For a recent look at the purpose of the gospel, see D. A. Carson, "The Purpose of the Fourth Gospel: John 20:31 Reconsidered," *JBL* 106 (1987) 639–51. Carson concludes that, contrary to the opinion of most recent scholarship, the gospel may in fact have an evangelistic intent.

[40] See Brown, *Community*, 13–24.

[41] Similar inclusion of the implied readers and those real readers who see themselves as addressed by the gospel is to be found in 4:48, which castigates not only the centurion but "you" plural [$\H{\iota}\delta\eta\tau\epsilon$] for requiring signs and wonders in order to believe, and in 20:29, in which Jesus gently rebukes Thomas, "Have you believed because you have seen me? Blessed are those who have not seen and yet believe."

[42] For a good summary of these moves, see Steven Mailloux, "Learning to Read: Interpretation and Reader-Response Criticism," *Studies in the Literary Imagination* 12 (1979) 93–108; Mailloux, *Rhetorical Power* (Ithaca: Cornell University Press, 1989) 39–53.

[43] Iser is challenged on this point by Terry Eagleton, who labels this notion an "arbitrary prejudice." Where Iser appears, to the present reader, to be making a statement concerning the psychology of reading ("readers strive for coherence"), Eagleton accuses him of delivering an

the process of grouping together all the different aspects of a text to form the consistency that the reader will always be in search of. While expectations may be continually modified, and images continually expanded, the reader will still strive, even if unconsciously, to fit everything together in a consistent pattern.[44]

In their efforts at consistency building, readers, implied and real, utilize two sets of data in responding to and making sense of a given text.[45] They use data intrinsic to the text, following the clues of the text in order to fill in the gaps between words, sentences, paragraphs, chapters, and ideas within the text. They also bring extrinsic data to the text, including cultural, linguistic, biographical, and other information from outside the world of the text.[46] These extrinsic data contribute to the "horizon of expectations" which the implied reader (as well as the real reader) will bring to the text. Although the horizon of expectations is not controlled by the implied author, that author, through the narrative itself, can manipulate, frustrate, or modify it in order to create an effect on the reader.[47]

Although both real and implied readers apply intrinsic and extrinsic data to their readings, a real reader will not read the text in the same way that the implied reader is expected to do. On the contrary, a given real reader's reading, while using the same intrinsic data as are available to the implied reader and perhaps even identifying with the implied reader, will depend to some degree on the purpose for which he or she is reading the text, as well as on the specific extrinsic data which he or she brings to bear on a reading of the text. For example, many Christian readers of the gospels are interested in deriving some

---

authoritarian instruction to the readers, that they "*must* construct the text so as to render it internally consistent" (emphasis added). For Eagleton's critique of Iser and other reader-response critics, see his *Literary Theory: An Introduction* (Oxford: Basil Blackwell, 1983) 61–90.

[44] Iser, *Implied Reader*, 283.

[45] Ibid., 284.

[46] It is the ever-presence of extrinsic data—information, biases, points of view—which readers inevitably bring to the text which is responsible for "subjectivity," an element which reader-response critics, as well as other sorts of literary critics, have difficulty taking into account. For one critic's attempt to do so, see Stanley Fish, *Is there a Text in this Class?* (Cambridge: Harvard University Press, 1980) 1–17.

[47] For discussion of "horizon of expectations," see Hans Robert Jauss, "Literary History as a Challenge to Literary Theory," *New Literary History* 2 (1970–71) 7–31, and *idem*, "Theses on the Transition from the Aesthetics of Literary Works to a Theory of Aesthetic Experience," *Interpretation of Narrative* (ed. Mario J. Valdés and Owen Miller; Toronto: University of Toronto Press, 1978) 140–41.

guidance for their lives in the present.[48] On the other hand, Jewish readers may be interested in learning about the symbols and images used by their Christian friends, or in investigating the issue of anti-Judaism in the gospels.[49]

When New Testament exegetes read the text, it is often with a view to determining the "meaning" of the text for its original audience. This entails, whether explicitly or implicitly, the process of reconstructing the way in which the implied readers might have read the text, that is, filled in the gaps left by the narrator/implied author. This task in itself points out yet another kind of gap, which is the very real distance in time, space, and cultural milieu, which exists between the exegete and the implied reader inscribed in the gospel narratives. This last gap, perhaps more appropriately, this gulf, places the reader-response critical enterprise, as often practiced in the field of New Testament studies, in the service of historical-critical concerns.[50] Not only do these texts, and their implied authors, draw on the literary conventions, symbols, and norms of another age and another time to convey a message to the implied readers, but those readers would do the same in decoding, that is, in reading and receiving the message of, the texts. The exegete attempts to take on the role of the implied reader as a receptor and decoder of the signals of the implied author encoded in the text.[51] In doing so, however, he or she also interacts with the work of other scholars, and generally attempts to set his or her work in the context of contemporary New Testament scholarship. The norms, assumptions, and language of scholarship therefore become elements in the extrinsic data which the exegete uses to interpret the gospels, even while the exegete is trying— whether implicitly or explicitly[52]—to reconstruct the implied reader's reading of the text at hand.

---

[48] For example, see Thomas Boomershine, *Story Journey: An Invitation to the Gospel as Storytelling* (Nashville: Abingdon, 1988).

[49] See Samuel Sandmel, *Anti-Semitism in the New Testament?* (Philadelphia: Fortress, 1978); Adele Reinhartz, "The New Testament and Anti-Judaism: A Literary-Critical Approach," *JES* 25 (1988) 524–37.

[50] Moore (*Literary Criticism*, 72), suggests that "recent literary exegesis of the Gospels...has found this reader-in-the text approach especially congenial." For this reason, "New Testament reader-response criticism is a more narrowly focused and more unified phenomenon than its nonbiblical counterpart."

[51] This is impossible to do in any complete way, as it is difficult if not impossible for modern readers, including exegetes, to put aside completely their own concerns and reading strategies. This may be part of what underlies the view of Iser (*The Implied Reader*, xii), who sees the implied reader as a blend between the reader inherent in the text and the real reader who responds to the text. He states that "this term incorporates both the prestructuring of the potential meaning by the text, and the reader's actualization of this potential through the reading process."

[52] This focus on the implied reader, in his or her guise as the intended audience, is not the exclusive province of reader-response critics. Rather, the entire corpus of New Testament

The present study of the Gospel of John will focus primarily on intrinsic data, that is, on the clues provided within the gospel itself. This is not done out of imitation of New Critics, who see every text as a closed entity requiring no outside information for its interpretation.[53] Rather, this focus on the text reflects what Wayne Meeks has called "the self-referring quality of the whole Gospel, [which is a] closed system of metaphors."[54] In making sense of this closed world, the real reader, to a certain degree at least, is on the same footing as the implied reader, since both must rely primarily on the information gleaned from the text itself.

Furthermore, although the narrative sequence of the gospel, that is, the order in which ideas, events, and metaphors are presented, is important for its interpretation and will be one of the principal elements of the narrative used by readers to construct coherent meaning,[55] the gospel itself leaves the way open for a holistic reading as well. Whereas in a first reading the readers' expectations are continually challenged and revised as they proceed sequentially through the text, upon rereading the same text, readers are influenced not only by the narrative sequence but also by material from the text as a whole.

While some genres, such as mystery novels, are aimed primarily at the first-time reader, the gospels are intended by their implied authors to be read and reread many times. This is surmised from the fact that in almost every case the reader is given information at the end of the gospel which prompts a re-

---

scholarship is testimony to the centrality, and the difficulty, of this endeavor. See, for example, Paul S. Minear, *John, The Martyr's Gospel* (New York: Pilgrims, 1984) 14–23.

[53] For an introduction to New Criticism, see Eagleton, *Literary Theory*, 47–53.

[54] Meeks, "Man from Heaven," 68. Although the generally self-referential nature of this gospel focuses attention on the gospel itself as the primary resource for the exegesis of a given passage, it also points beyond itself on occasion. There are clear references and allusions not only to biblical passages, but also to events and ideas which were apparently known from other sources, literary or non-literary. For example, 3:24 implies that the imprisonment of John the Baptist was common knowledge, though it is not recounted in this gospel. Similarly, 7:42 creates dramatic irony by referring to Bethlehem as the birthplace of the Messiah, another detail not mentioned in this gospel. Furthermore, many of the terms used in the gospel, while given particular Johannine definitions and nuances, were apparently part of the thought world shared by both author and intended audience. This is especially clear with regard to the christological titles such as Logos, Christ, Son of Man, Son of God, Prophet, and King of Israel. In exegeting the Fourth Gospel, many scholars do take seriously the extra-Johannine background, but give precedence to intra-textual factors. See, for example, Schnackenburg, "Excursus III: The Titles of Jesus in John 1," Schnack. 1.507–14.

[55] On the importance of sequential reading, see Iser, *Implied Reader*, 278.

evaluation of the entire gospel.[56] In the case of the Fourth Gospel, this information is found in 20:30–31.

These verses are not only a fitting conclusion to a sequential reading of the gospel[57] but also serve as an invitation to reread the gospel in light of the perspective expressed in them.[58] Although the narrator has provided clues regarding the "correct" interpretation of the signs narratives throughout the course of his narration, in 20:30–31 the reader is addressed directly and told of the implied author's reason for telling his story, namely, to encourage christological understanding, which leads to faith and eternal life. This perspective will inform the reader's second and subsequent encounters with the text. As Iser notes,

> In every text there is a potential time sequence which the reader must inevitably realize, as it is impossible to absorb even a short text in a single moment. Thus the reading process always involves viewing the text through a perspective that is continually on the move, linking up the different phases, and so constructing what we have called the virtual dimension. This dimension, of course, varies all the time we are reading. However, when we have finished the text, and read it again, clearly our extra knowledge will result in a different time sequence; we shall tend to establish connections by referring to our awareness of what is to come, and so certain aspects of the text will assume a significance we did not attach to them on a first reading, while others will recede into the background.[59]

---

[56] See Mark 16:1–9, in which the "messianic secret" is finally revealed, Matt 28:20, in which the Risen Lord asks his disciples to teach others "to observe all that I have commanded you," including, presumably, Jesus' commandments as recorded in the First Gospel, and Luke 24:45, in which the Risen Lord opens the minds of his disciples to understand the scriptures, as well as Jesus' words (24:44). In these passages, the messages imparted to characters within the narratives affect the implied readers, who can now reread the texts in the light of their new insight.

[57] In this study we will accept the viewpoint of a majority of Johannine scholars that chapter 21 is an epilogue to the body of the text. See AB 2.1077–82 for detailed discussion. Since the gospel apparently did not circulate without chapter 21, however, it would have been read by the implied readers and utilized in making sense of the gospel as a whole. This would not, however, detract from the force of 20:30–31 as the conclusion and statement of purpose conveyed by the implied author to the implied reader. Indeed, the concluding verse of chapter 21 would not replace 20:30–31 but, by repeating that the function of the book was to record a selection of Jesus' acts, would rather serve to remind the reader of the earlier passage.

[58] This would have been reinforced by the liturgy, if the gospels were already read during worship at this time. For a historical survey of the role of the Bible in liturgy, see S. J. P. van Dijk, "The Bible in Liturgical Use," *The Cambridge History of the Bible* (ed. G. W. H. Lampe; Cambridge: Cambridge University Press, 1969) 2.220–52 .

[59] Iser, *Implied Reader*, 280–81.

There are other indications of the implied author's anticipation of multiple readings of the text on the part of the implied reader. In 11:2, for example, the reader is told of an event—Mary's anointing of Jesus—which is described in chapter 12. Furthermore, the gospel emphasizes at several points that even the disciples did not understand the full import of Jesus' words upon first hearing them. In 2:22, we are told that the saying of Jesus recorded in 2:19 ("Destroy this temple, and in three days I will raise it up") was remembered, and presumably understood, by the disciples only after Jesus' resurrection. The comprehension of Jesus' words will also be aided by the paraclete, who, according to 14:26, "will...remind you of all that I have said to you." If the disciples, who had the privilege of being eye-witnesses to the works and words of Jesus, did not comprehend everything first time around (cf. 16:28–29), surely the implied readers of the gospel would not have been expected to do so. For this reason, while attention will be paid in the present study to sequential features of the text, material will be considered out of narrative sequence as well.

As a real reader, what I offer in this study is my own reading, my own attempt to reconstruct the reading experience of the implied reader as it pertains to the gospel story. The study will of necessity have points of contact with both formalism, because of its focus on constructs inherent in the text itself, and historical criticism, since it is concerned primarily with the implied reader and only secondarily with a specialized group of contemporary readers of this ancient text, namely New Testament exegetes. Yet it is unrealistic and artificial to attempt to isolate reader-response criticism from other kinds of concerns. Indeed, it would seem that one of the important contributions of reader-response criticism to New Testament studies is a greater clarity on the reading strategies not only of ancient readers but of contemporary readers including New Testament exegetes themselves. Included among these strategies is the necessity to construct and engage the implied reader in the course of one's reading and exegesis of the text. As Stephen Moore suggests, "to read any literary text...is always in some sense to read through its reader construct, to dialogue with it, and through it to dialogue with its author construct."[60] For this reason, the reading of the implied reader, which is the focus of the present and many other reader-oriented gospel studies, should not be seen in contrast to the readings of contemporary readers, but rather as one of the factors constitutive of those readings.

It is my hope that the reading which I offer in these pages will help to illuminate the attempts of other readers to read this most enigmatic of gospels in a meaningful way.

---

[60] Stephen Moore, *Literary Criticism*, 72.

The study will begin in chapter one by looking in detail at the cosmological tale as it comes to expression in this gospel. The tale will be reconstructed on the basis of the clues or signals of the gospel narrative, and its identity as a tale will be explored. Chapter two will examine the role of the cosmological tale in the narrative strategy of the Johannine narrator as well as its effect on the reader. The remainder of the study will focus on one particular passage as a more detailed test case of the way in which the implied reader may have used the cosmological tale as an interpretive key. The passage is the παροιμία (*paroimia*)—cryptic discourse or riddle—of the Shepherd and the Sheep in John 10:1–5. Accordingly, the third chapter will provide a survey of scholarly attempts to solve this riddle, most of which have understood it in the context of the historical and/or ecclesiological tales. The fourth chapter will develop a cosmological reading of the passage based on clues within the Fourth Gospel. The study will conclude by examining the implications of the study for our understanding of Johannine literary technique on the one hand, and the historical situation of the implied audience on the other. Finally, in an appendix, we will examine relevant material from outside the gospel which may provide insight into some of the extrinsic data which implied readers may have brought to their reading of the *paroimia*.

1

THE COSMOLOGICAL TALE

The presence of the cosmological tale in the Fourth Gospel is signalled to the reader in the very first verse. Like the Gospels of Matthew and Luke, the Gospel of John prefaces its account of Jesus' ministry with a "narrative of origins,"[1] and like the Gospel of Mark, John begins at the beginning (ἐν ἀρχῇ). But unlike its synoptic counterparts, the Fourth Gospel presents Jesus' origins in cosmic terms, by telling of the pre-existent Word of God who became flesh in order to dwell in the world.

The cosmic beginning to this gospel is remarked upon by virtually every commentator. Echoed by many is Lindars' observation that in the prologue, "John has felt it desirable to place Jesus in the cosmic setting of his relationship to the Father, which is everywhere presupposed but not treated systematically."[2] What have not been sufficiently noted, however, are the narrative properties of this introduction. The prologue is not simply a hymn[3] or a "cultic-liturgical poem"[4] comprised of cosmological statements about the origins of the Word, but is itself a brief narrative about the Word and its relationship to the world. As such, it provides the reader with a précis of the cosmological tale. The prologue not only summarizes the main divisions of the gospel and introduces some of its major themes and characters,[5] but it also acts as the reader's guide to the cosmological tale as it comes to expression throughout the body of the gospel narrative.

---

[1] Segovia, "Journey," 35.

[2] Barnabas Lindars, *The Gospel of John,* (New Century Bible Commentary; Grand Rapids: Eerdmans, 1972) 76. See also AB 1.18. Lindars' argument that the prologue was not part of the first edition of the gospel (Lindars, *Gospel,* 76–77) is not shared by all. For discussion, see AB 1.19–21.

[3] Schnack. 1.223; Lindars, *Gospel,* 81.

[4] Bultmann, 14.

[5] AB 1.19.

THE COSMOLOGICAL TALE AS TOLD IN THE PROLOGUE

The prologue begins by describing the Word as pre-existent (1:1).[6] As a partner in God's creation of the world (1:3), the Word existed before the creation of the world, in that non-worldly realm which God also inhabits (1:1). In this phase of the Word's relations with the world, therefore, we see the Word as existing before the creation of the world, being instrumental in its creation, and continuing to exist in some non-worldly realm after the world's creation is complete.

The second phase is the Word's entry into the world. It is anticipated by John the Baptist, who bears witness to the "light," an alternate description of the "Word." The entry is described explicitly in 1:9: "The true light, which enlightens everyone, was coming into the world." Verses 1:10–13 illustrate two possible responses to the light, namely, rejection and acceptance, and indicate that a positive response of receiving and believing results in a transformation of the believer: "But to all who received him, who believed in his name, he gave power to become children of God" (1:12). Verses 1:14–18 reinforce the idea of the Word's entry into the world and its significance for humankind: "And the Word became flesh and lived among us…" (1:14); "From his fullness have we all received, grace upon grace" (1:16).

Finally, the Word's departure from the world is implied in 1:18. This verse refers to the general purpose of the Word's activity in the world, which is to make the Father known to the world. It also implies the Word's departure from the world, by referring to the Son in the present tense as being close to (New RSV) or in the bosom of (RSV) the Father (εἰς τὸν κόλπον τοῦ πατρὸς).[7]

This description of the cosmological tale as told in the prologue focuses on the temporal order of events as encountered in a sequential reading of the prologue. The main concern of this temporal sequence is to delineate a spatial

---

[6] The idea of the Word's pre-existence is thought by many scholars to be an indication of the presence of Wisdom christology in the gospel. See, for example, Elizabeth A. Johnson, "Jesus, the Wisdom of God: A Biblical Basis for a Non-Androcentric Christianity," *ETL* 61 (1985) 284–9; Dodd, 295; Ignace de la Potterie, "La Verita in San Giovanni," *RivB* 11 (1963) 3–24 (reprinted in Ashton, 53–66); T. H. Tobin, "The Prologue of John and Hellenistic Jewish Speculation," *CBQ* 52 (1990) 252–69; John Ashton, "The Transformation of Wisdom: A Study of the Prologue of John's Gospel," *NTS* 32 (1986) 161–86.

[7] The precise meaning of the Greek is difficult to determine. While Ernst Haenchen (*John 1: A Commentary on the Gospel of John Chapter 1–6* [Philadelphia: Fortress, 1984] 121) argues that the present participle ὁ ὤν has a past connotation here, it may be argued that one should take the present sense seriously to indicate that at the time of writing the Son is with the Father as he was before the incarnation. In support of this view, see I. de la Potterie, "C'est lui qui a ouvert la voie: la finale du prologue johannique," *Bib* 69 (1988) 340–370. For a survey of background material to this phrase, see Schnack. 1.280–81.

relationship, that is, the relationship between the Word and the world. All of the events emphasize one aspect or another of this spatial relationship. Hence it may be said that this tale describes the movement of its central character, Jesus, through time and space.

Several further conclusions regarding the cosmological tale can be drawn from the prologue. First, the Word is the Son of the Father. Second, his entry into the world served a specific purpose, described as making the Father known and enlightening the world (1:9). Third, his coming engendered the desired positive response among many, who as a result enjoyed benefits such as becoming children of God and receiving grace upon grace. Not all, however accepted him, implying the presence of a conflict in which Jesus is ultimately victorious (cf. 1:5). Fourth, the prologue is narrated retrospectively, from a point in time after the Son's return to the Father. Finally, the tone and especially the use of the first person plural in 1:14 and 1:16 indicate clearly the perspective or point of view of the narrator as the voice of the implied author, who thereby includes himself among those who have beheld the glory of the Word. This constitutes an invitation to the implied reader to do the same.

The Fourth Gospel therefore introduces its readers to the gospel narrative by providing not merely a description of Jesus' cosmic origins but by telling a brief tale of the Word's relationship with the world. In this tale, as it comes to expression in the prologue, the spatial and temporal elements are prominent. The temporal element is signaled by expressions such as "in the beginning" (1:1), and verb forms, such as the present participle $\dot{\epsilon}\rho\chi\dot{o}\mu\epsilon\nu o\varsigma$ (1:9). The spatial element is marked by verbs such as $\tilde{\eta}\lambda\theta\epsilon\nu$ (1:11), $\dot{\epsilon}\gamma\dot{\epsilon}\nu\epsilon\tau o$ (1:14) and $\dot{\epsilon}\sigma\kappa\dot{\eta}\nu\omega\sigma\epsilon\nu$ (1:14), and describes the Word's location vis-à-vis the world or $\kappa\dot{o}\sigma\mu o\varsigma$ (1:9, 10). Hence it may be said that the plot of this story revolves around the relationship in time of the Word and the world.

THE COSMOLOGICAL TALE IN THE GOSPEL NARRATIVE

Although there has been some debate concerning the precise break between the prologue and the next section of the gospel,[8] from a narrative perspective 1:19 clearly begins a new section. In recounting in detail the testimony of John the Baptist (alluded to in 1:6–8), 1:19–34 begins the narrative of the historical tale proper. But although the explicit cosmological language of the prologue has

---

8 Segovia ("Journeys," 35), among others, also sees 1:18 as the conclusion to the first section of the gospel. Others, however, such as Lindars (Gospel, 76), argue that the first section extends to 2:12. For further discussion, see AB 1.19.

been temporarily left behind,[9] the testimony of John the Baptist is also, according to the summary provided in the prologue, the beginning of the second phase of the cosmological tale, namely, Jesus' activity in the world. The character of John the Baptist, therefore, has a dual function. He is the one who identifies the Word as Jesus and presents his testimony to the human characters within the historical tale. He is also the one who signals the Word's arrival in the world, within the cosmological tale. This second phase continues until the passion narrative, during which Jesus is crucified (within the historical tale) and the Word returns to the Father (within the cosmological tale). In this way, as Segovia and Kysar have also noted, the cosmological tale proceeds parallel to the historical tale.[10]

The ties between the cosmological tale in the prologue and the Fourth Gospel narrative as a whole run much deeper than such general structural parallels. In fact, the structure and language of the cosmological tale outlined in the prologue provide the reader with two keys to discerning a much more detailed version of this tale in the gospel as a whole.

The first key is the temporal relationships among the various phases of the cosmological tale. For example, references to Jesus' pre-existence, though scattered throughout the body of the gospel,[11] would be understood in the context of the pre-existent Word as described in the prologue. References to Jesus' departure from the world and his return to the Father (16:10, 28) would be associated with the final phase of the cosmological tale as told in the prologue, when the Son is in the bosom of the Father once more (1:18).

The second key is the use throughout the gospel of spatial language which echoes the spatial relationships set out in the prologue. In the prologue, the world is the space with reference to which the Word's activities are described. The Word moves from a location outside of the world, into the world, and then out again. The body of the gospel contains many similar spatial references, particularly in the discourse sections. These include the contrast between above and below (3:31; 8:23), heaven and earth (3:12–13, 31), ascent and descent (3:13). Although these pairs serve to describe Jesus' spatial activity more precisely than does the prologue, they all have the "world" as their frame of reference. Therefore it may be suggested that the cosmological tale outlined in the prologue may be fleshed out in greater detail by examining the passages in which the term κόσμος occurs.

---

[9] Although "Logos" is not used as a christological term after the prologue, many other concepts introduced in the prologue and related to the cosmological tale appear throughout the gospel. See AB 1.19.

[10] See AB 1.19.

[11] For example, 8:58; 17:5.

The Fourth Gospel abounds in references to Jesus' relationship to the "world." Commentators are quick to point out the obvious, namely that the term κόσμος is actually used in this gospel in different ways and with different nuances, depending on the context in which it appears.[12] While these distinctions are important for an interpretation of the Johannine view of the "world" and the varied functions of the term in the gospel narrative as well as in Johannine theology, they should not obscure the heuristic function of the word itself. To illustrate this point, it will be helpful to look at each component of the tale individually. Detailed explorations of each of these points have been provided by many scholars for different purposes. Our examination will therefore be brief and will focus on the role of each component in the plot of the cosmological tale. Furthermore, it will also be holistic, on the assumption that on rereading the gospel, readers will organize references from the entire gospel within the framework of the cosmological tale as outlined in the prologue.

PHASE ONE: PRE-EXISTENCE

In addition to the prologue, Jesus' pre-existence is mentioned specifically in chapter 17. John 17:5 refers to the glory which Jesus had with the Father before the world existed. Similarly, 17:24 speaks of the glory which the Father has given the Son "before the foundation of the world." A hint of the idea that Jesus existed before his entry into the world may also be found in 8:58, in which Jesus declares: "Very truly, I tell you, before Abraham was, I am."[13]

PHASE TWO: JESUS IN THE WORLD

Jesus' entry into the world. This event is described in different ways in many passages throughout the gospel. In 9:39, Jesus speaks of his coming into the world in the first person: "I came into this world for judgment...." Verses 3:19, 8:12, 12:46, among others, echo the language of the prologue by referring to Jesus as he who has come into the world. In the Bread of Life discourse (6:25–71), Jesus refers to himself as "the bread of God...which comes down from heaven and gives life to the world" (6:33).

The concepts of consecration and mission which are implicit in the Bread of Life discourse are expressed directly in many verses which declare that Jesus has been sent into the world by the Father (3:17; 10:36; 11:42; 17:21, 23). In

---

12 See, for example, Kysar, *Fourth Evangelist*, 242; Ernst Käsemann, *The Testament of Jesus* (Philadelphia: Fortress, 1968) 63.
13 See Schnack. 2.223.

10:36, Jesus speaks of himself as the one "whom the Father has sanctified and sent into the world." The claim that Jesus has been sent by God his Father is an integral part of the Father-Son relationship which in turn is one of the central building blocks of Johannine christology.[14]

Jesus' activity in the world. Jesus' activity while in the world is expressed in many ways. In 1:29, this activity is described by John the Baptist as taking away the sins of the world. More commonly, the narrator describes it as saving the world (3:17): "Indeed, God did not send the Son into the world to condemn the world, but in order that the world might be saved through him." This passage implies that this soteriological activity was indeed the purpose for which the Son entered the world (cf. 8:42).

There are two images which predominate in passages which speak of Jesus' activity and presence in the world. The first is the image of light. In the prologue (1:9) Jesus is described as the light who has come into the world. This metaphor is repeated explicitly in 12:46, as Jesus reaches the end of his mission in the world: "I have come as light into the world, so that everyone who believes in me should not remain in the darkness." It also surfaces at points in between, as in 8:12 and 11:9–10.

Closely connected with the imagery of light is that of life. As Jesus tells the Jews in 8:12: "I am the light of the world. Whoever follows me will never walk in darkness, but will have the light of life." Elsewhere the "life" image—to be understood as "eternal life"[15]—is used in conjunction with other metaphors, as in 6:33: "For the bread of God is that which comes down from heaven and gives life to the world." The term "Son" could be substituted for bread here, since it is clear that it is Jesus, the Son of God, who is the bread of life (6:35).

The bread of life discourse also expresses the purpose of Jesus' arrival in the world in a more general way: "for I have come down from heaven, not to do my own will, but the will of him who sent me..." (6:38). The passage continues to make this will more explicit: "and this is the will of him who sent me, that I should lose nothing of all that he has given me, but raise it up on the last day" (6:39).

Another purpose for Jesus' activity in the world is judgment, though exactly what is meant by this is not clear. In 9:39, Jesus claims, "I came into this world for judgment, so that those who do not see may see, and those who do see may

---

[14] For a discussion of the background of this concept in agent christology, see Peder Borgen, "God's Agent in the Fourth Gospel," *Religions in Antiquity* (ed. Jacob Neusner; Leiden: Brill, 1968) 67–78 (reprinted in Ashton, 67–78).

[15] See the study by J. G. van der Watt, "The use of αἰώνιος in the concept ζωή αἰώνιος in John's Gospel," *NovT* 31 (1989) 217–28.

become blind." This passage draws a thematic connection between judgment and light: to bring judgment is also in some sense to bring light into the world, and to judge people according to whether they see the light or not. In 12:47b, however, Jesus apparently contradicts this, stating that "I came not to judge the world, but to save the world." In this latter verse, the term judgment seems to be equivalent to condemnation and expresses the wish that the world as a whole might be saved.[16]

Finally, implicit in all passages depicting Jesus' purpose in the world is the claim that he comes to gather followers. These followers by definition are those who believe in Jesus (1:43), see the light, are saved, and are destined to be raised to eternal life. This purpose is clear in all of the passages which talk about following Jesus and believing him (e.g. 1:43), as well as those which depict the call of disciples and other followers (e.g. 1:35–51). It is also the explicit concern of chapter 17, in which Jesus states that he has fulfilled the mission, that is, "I have made your name known to those whom you gave me from the world. They were yours, and you gave them to me, and they have kept your word" (17:6).

In all of the passages discussed thus far, the emphasis is on the soteriological function of Jesus in his worldly activity. Yet there is another element to his presence which is hinted at in some of these passages and comes to more explicit expression in others. This is the element of conflict. The gospel discusses conflict between Jesus and others in two ways. In the first place, it is clear from the prologue that there is resistance on the part of the "world" to Jesus' message, and indeed to his very presence in the world. As 1:10 states, "He was in the world, and the world came into being through him, yet the world did not know him." This is also expressed in other passages which speak of the world's resistance to and hatred of Jesus, such as 7:7, in which Jesus tells his brothers, "The world cannot hate you, but it hates me because I testify against it that its works are evil."

Yet it is not only the world (16:33) and its darkness (1:5) which Jesus must overcome, but also an antagonist whom the gospel describes as "the ruler of this world" or the evil one. Jesus warns his disciples,"I will no longer talk much with you, for the ruler of this world is coming. He has no power over me; but I do as the Father has commanded me, so that the world may know that I love the Father" (14:30–31). In 16:11 Jesus declares that the ruler of this world is judged. In 17:15, Jesus prays to the Father not to take his followers out of the world, but to keep them from the evil one. That there is identity, or at least some connection, between the ruler of this world and the evil one is implied in this

---

16 For a detailed study of the judgment theme, see Josef Blank, *Krisis: Untersuchungen zur johanneischen Christologie und Eschatologie* (Freiburg: Lambertus, 1964).

verse. The followers who remain in the world need protection from the evil one who presumably exerts power in the world. Although the gospel is not explicit about the identity of the ruler of this world, it is generally thought to be Satan or the devil (cf. 8:44).[17]

Jesus' statements in 16:33 and 16:11 imply his victory over the ruler of this world. This might also be behind his statement about kingship at his trial. When asked by Pilate whether he is King of the Jews (18:33), Jesus responds: "My kingship is not from this world" (18:36). This suggests that he is the ruler that is not of this world, who has vanquished the ruler of this world.

PHASE THREE: JESUS' DEPARTURE FROM THE WORLD

The final element of the plot is the departure of Jesus from the world, which also constitutes his final victory over the ruler of this world and the end of his personal activity in the world. The crucifixion and resurrection events act as the vehicle for his departure. But this departure has been anticipated as part of the overall plan and has been hinted at long before the passion events are told. For example, in 7:33–34, Jesus tells the Jews: "I will be with you a little while longer, and then I am going to him who sent me. You will search for me, but you will not find me; and where I am, you cannot come."[18] In 9:4–5, Jesus implies that he is not in the world permanently: "We must work the works of him who sent me, while it is day; night is coming, when no one can work. As long as I am in the world, I am the light of the world." In 13:1, the narrator reflects on Jesus' knowledge that the time had come for him to depart out of this world to the Father. Jesus refers to this in his prayer in 17:11: "And now I am no longer in the world...."

In several passages, Jesus' return to the Father is described as an ascent.[19] In 3:13, he declares to Nicodemus: "No one has ascended into heaven but the one who descended from heaven, the Son of Man." In 6:61–62, he challenges those who doubt him, "Does this offend you? Then what if you were to see the Son of Man ascending to where he was before?" Verse 20:17 catches Jesus in that moment between resurrection and ascension, in which Jesus tells Mary Magdalene, "Do not hold onto me, because I have not yet ascended to the Father. But go to my brothers and say to them, 'I am ascending to my Father and your Father, to my God and your God.' "[20]

---

[17] See discussion in chapter four, pages 91–92 below.

[18] Cf. 8:14.

[19] The language of ascent and descent is seen as fundamental to Johannine christology by many scholars; see, e.g., Meeks, "Man from Heaven."

[20] For discussion of various interpretations, see AB 2.992–93.

The ascension passages indicate that this departure from the world is a return to the situation that Jesus enjoyed before entering into the world. As such it completes the circle of activity that began with his pre-existent creation. There are several hints, however, that the circle is not completely closed: the cosmological tale is not entirely completed by Jesus' departure.

The first hint that Jesus' relationship with the "world" is not yet at an end is to be found in the language in which Jesus describes the future work of his disciples. According to 17:18, Jesus sends his followers out into the world just as the Father had sent him out. From the context it would appear that the followers are sent out in order to continue Jesus' work of spreading the word of God and gathering disciples. Chapter 17 as a whole makes it clear that those who are gathered by the disciples also have a place in Jesus' prayer to the Father and will be among those who are saved and resurrected to eternal life (5:29). The actual commissioning of the disciples to carry on Jesus' work takes place in 20:21-23, during Jesus' first resurrection appearance to the disciples: "Peace be with you. As the Father has sent me, so I send you.... Receive the Holy Spirit. If you forgive the sins of any, they are forgiven; if you retain the sins of any, they are retained."[21]

The second hint is found in the references to the paraclete. This figure takes over Jesus' role in the world. The paraclete, like Jesus, will be sent by the Father (14:26a; cf. 15:26)[22] and will continue Jesus' mission by teaching the followers as well as by reminding them of Jesus' words (14:26b). The paraclete will also act as a witness to Jesus (15:26) and convince the world concerning sin and righteousness and judgment (16:8) just as Jesus had done when in the world. According to 16:7, the coming of the paraclete is dependent upon Jesus' departure from the world. In this verse, Jesus tells the disciples: "it is to your advantage that I go away, for if I do not go away, the Advocate [ὁ παράκλητος] will not come to you; but if I go, I will send him to you."

The third hint concerns the situation of the followers and disciples whom Jesus gathered while in the world. In 14:2-3, Jesus promises to return and take them to his Father's house, where he is now going to prepare a place for them. Hence Jesus' departure and separation from his disciples are not for eternity; his followers have hopes of being with him again in the realm where he now is (cf. also 13:36; 14:19).[23] From these hints it may be inferred that the temporal

---

21 For discussion, see D. A. Carson, *The Gospel According to John* (Grand Rapids: Eerdmans, 1991) 647-49.

22 For detailed discussion of the paraclete in the Fourth Gospel, see George Johnston, *The Spirit-Paraclete in the Gospel of John* (Cambridge: Cambridge University Press, 1970).

23 Robert Kysar (*John, the Maverick Gospel* [Atlanta: John Knox, 1976] 89) follows Käsemann in defining 14:2-3 as "heavenly eschatology." The precise relationship between this

framework of the cosmological tale does not end with Jesus' ascension or with the close of the Johannine narrative, but will properly be completed with Jesus' return—the *parousia*—and the resurrection of his followers. In the meantime, the paraclete acts as Jesus' representative in the world, while Jesus' disciples, in continuing his work, are his agents.

NARRATOR'S POINT OF VIEW

The implied author is writing in the period of time between Jesus' ascension and his return, that is, during the time when the paraclete has arrived and the disciples are carrying out their mission while awaiting the *parousia*. This is suggested in particular by two passages which, though attributed to the Johannine Jesus, reflect the post-ascension perspective of the implied author. The first is chapter 17, in which those who have come to faith through the words of the disciples are explicitly embraced in Jesus' prayer (17:20). The second is 20:29, in which the Johannine Jesus, looking over the heads of the characters of the gospel narrative towards its readers, gently rebukes Thomas: "Have you believed because you have seen me? Blessed are those who have not seen and yet have come to believe."

Throughout the gospel, in narrative and in discourse, it is clear that the implied author through the voices of the Johannine Jesus and the narrator expresses the perspective of those who believe and follow Jesus and thus see themselves as "having life in his name." This is apparent from the positive language associated with belief and the negative language associated with disbelief, as illustrated, for example, in 3:17–18:[24]

> Indeed, God did not send the Son into the world in order to condemn the world, but in order that the world might be saved through him. Those who believe in him are not condemned; but those who do not believe are condemned already, because they have not believed in the name of the only Son of God.

---

type of eschatology and the present and future eschatologies in evidence elsewhere in the gospel is not clear. However, this passage fits in well with the cosmological tale, in that it uses spatial language to express an eschatological viewpoint.

[24] There is some ambiguity as to the speaker of these words. AB 1.149, as well as the editors of the *New Revised Standard Version*, consider Jesus to be the speaker. Schnackenburg (Schnack. 1.390) considers these to be the words of the evangelist, i.e., the narrator.

It is also illustrated in the signs narratives, in which the problem experienced by an individual or group is alleviated by Jesus in response to, or as a prelude to, faith. For example, after the wedding at Cana, during which Jesus turned water into wine, the disciples, we are told, believed in him (2:12). Similarly, the healing of the official's son (4:46–53) is integrally related to the faith of the official and his entire household (4:50, 54). The readers are therefore encouraged by the words of Jesus and the narrator, as well as by the paradigms of belief presented by other characters, to accept the perspective of the implied author in the hope of being themselves included in that group which will have life in his name.[25]

Through the passages which speak of the "world" and Jesus' relationship to it, we can discern the story of the Son of God who existed with the Father before the foundation of the world. He was sent by the Father into the world in order to save its inhabitants from sin, darkness, and the diabolical "ruler of this world." The Son met some resistance among the very people to whom he was sent, but he did succeed in fulfilling his divinely-given mission with respect to a dedicated group of followers. Meeting and vanquishing death through his own crucifixion and resurrection, he returned to the Father. This return did not mark the end of his relationship with the world, for he promised to maintain this relationship by sending the paraclete to the believers and by sending out the disciples. Finally, he promised to return, to lead his followers to the realm of the Father.

CONCLUSION

In this chapter we have argued that the implied reader would a) discern the outline of a three–part cosmological tale in the prologue to this gospel, and b) use this outline as a means of organizing the other discussions of Jesus and the world throughout the gospel into a coherent and more detailed version of the cosmological tale.

But is the narrative sequence that we have outlined a "tale"? A full discussion of the myriad definitions and descriptions of "story" in literary theory is beyond the scope of this study. Nevertheless, a few comments are necessary in order to support the claim that the schema which we have outlined would be perceived by the reader as a tale or story told by the narrator alongside the historical and ecclesiological tales.

---

25 The Johannine view of signs-faith has been much discussed. See, for example, Kysar, *Maverick Gospel*, 65–83; Sebald Hofbeck, σημεῖον (Wurzburg: Vier Türme, 1966) passim; Helmut Wenz, "Sehen und Glauben bei Johannes," *TZ* 17 (1961) 17–25.

Most literary critics agree that two of the basic components of any story or tale are character and plot.[26] These two are integrally related, since the actions and events which comprise the plot require actors to carry them out. From our discussion of the cosmological tale, it is apparent that it has both characters and plot. The main character is Jesus, variously known and described as the Son of God, the Son of Man, the Christ, the Word, the light, and the life. Other characters are God the Father, who sent the Son into the world; the ruler of this world, against whom Jesus struggles; and the human beings who respond to Jesus by either accepting or rejecting his message.

The term "plot," like the "story" of which it is as a part, is more difficult to define; each literary critic seems to create his or her own definition.[27] Most, however, would agree that there are four essential features of plot: sequence, causality, unity, and affective power. Sequence refers to the ordering of events. According to Aristotle, a plot must have a beginning, a middle, and an end.[28] This is certainly true of the cosmological tale: it begins by describing Jesus' existence with the Father and continues by relating Jesus' activity in the world. Its immediate conclusion depicts his departure from the world, while its long-term conclusion describes the return of Christ to the world in the future.

Causality can be seen in the connections among the sequential components of the plot. The Father had a particular purpose in sending the Son into the world, a purpose which constitutes Jesus' mission in the world. The various deeds and words of Jesus in the world are directed toward achieving this purpose. Similarly, Jesus' departure from the world is due to the completion of the mission. His future return will benefit those who responded positively to his mission.

Necessary to the element of causality as a characteristic of plot is the presence of conflict. In fact, it may be said that without conflict and opposition, plot does not exist at all.[29] In the cosmological tale, the Son of God experiences conflict in his attempts to fulfill his mission in the world. Opposition comes from human beings resistant to his message as well as from the "ruler of this world." Jesus' departure from the world represents the resolution of this conflict, that is,

---

[26] C. Hugh Holman, *A Handbook to Literature* (New York: Macmillan, 1986) 378.

[27] See, for example, *A Dictionary of Modern Critical Terms* (ed. Roger Fowler; London: Routledge and Kegan Paul, 1973) 145; *The Harper Handbook to Literature* (ed. Northrop Frye; New York: Harper and Row, 1985) 352; M. H. Abrams, *Glossary*, 127–28; Culpepper, 79–80.

[28] *Poetics* 1450–51. This passage is the standard starting point for discussions of plot. See Abrams, *Glossary*, 129; *Harper Handbook*, 352; *Dictionary*, 145. For one of many translations and discussions, see Aristotle, *Aristotle's Poetics* (New York: University Press of America, 1961) 15, 92.

[29] Holman, *Handbook*, 379.

the pronouncement of judgement and condemnation upon those who resist him and the overthrowing of the ruler of this world.

The unity of the plot follows from the presence of causal relationships among the sequential components. The cosmological tale, though pieced together from the passages which depict Jesus' relationship with the world, is a single narrative thread, closely related to other narrative threads in this gospel. It exhibits coherence and closure, with the ending—at least, that part of it which is narrated in the gospel—corresponding in a satisfying way to the beginning of the tale.[30]

Finally, and perhaps most importantly, it has affective power; it engenders specific responses in the implied reader and, ideally, in real readers as well. Often these responses are implied or even dictated by the Johannine Jesus. For example, 16:7 describes the necessity of Jesus' departure, in order that the paraclete might be sent to the world. The implication is that his audience, his followers, should accept and be grateful for this departure because of the benefit they will enjoy because of it. More explicit are the words of Jesus describing the disciples' emotional responses to Jesus' death and departure: "Very truly, I tell you, you will weep and mourn, but the world will rejoice; you will have pain, but your pain will turn into joy....So you have pain now, but I will see you again, and your hearts will rejoice, and no one will take your joy from you" (16:20, 22).

More than merely manipulating the reader's emotional response to the central episodes of the historical tale, however, the cosmological tale, or rather its implied author, attempts a radical change in the christology as well as the self-understanding of the implied reader. The various ways in which it does so will be the subject of the following chapter.

---

30 Such alignment of beginning and end is characteristic of many stories, according to *Harper Handbook*, 442.

2

THE COSMOLOGICAL TALE
AND THE IMPLIED READER

The implied author is very explicit about the impact that he intends his book to have on the implied reader. In 20:30–31, he declares that he has written his book for two related reasons: in order that the reader may believe that Jesus is the Messiah, the Son of God; and in order that through believing, the reader may have life in his name. The passage also implies that these ends may be achieved through a particular reading of the signs "written in this book" (20:30). The Fourth Gospel is therefore intended to have an impact on the reader's thinking regarding Jesus, his activities, and his identity on the one hand, and regarding the reader's own place in the world on the other. As 20:30–31 intimates, these two aspects are intertwined: the intellectual knowledge of Jesus' christological identity cannot be separated from faith in Jesus as the Christ and Son of God, which in turn is a necessary precondition for the experience of eternal life.

These two elements are intertwined in the cosmological tale as well. The tale is christological in that it describes Jesus, his origins, and his relationship to the world; it also addresses the self-understanding of the reader by focusing on the world's response to Jesus as crucial to his mission and by conveying the point of view of the narrator or implied author, who speaks as one who has understood the historical tale correctly, has made a positive response to Jesus, and would persuade his readers to do the same.

But the cosmological tale is not merely another vehicle through which the implied author conveys his christology and describes the desired faith response on the part of the reader. Rather, it is a meta-text which serves three specific functions for the reader: first, it provides the context for the other major christological expressions in the gospel; second, it supplies the framework within which the implied reader is to situate himself or herself; third, it serves as the interpretive key for the "correct," that is, the implied author's, understanding of the signs narratives and indeed the entire historical tale of this gospel. In all these respects, the cosmological tale functions as the meta-tale with respect to the historical tale (the primary tale) and the ecclesiological tale (sub-tale). Each of these functions will now be considered briefly.

CHRISTOLOGY

Christology is the central theme of this gospel[1] and is expressed, either directly or indirectly, in virtually every verse. Through an examination of the major christological titles assigned to Jesus in this gospel as well as the ἐγώ εἰμί sayings, we shall argue that Johannine christology is ultimately rooted in the cosmological tale. This can be demonstrated specifically by looking at those verses in which these christological expressions are linked with κόσμος or other terms central to the cosmological tale.

Christological titles. The prologue of the gospel speaks of Jesus as the Logos. Whatever the specific background of this term, the prologue clearly associates it with Jesus' pre-existence as well as his role in the creation of the world, both of which can be situated in the context of the cosmological tale. Similarly, the Lamb of God title, which appears only in the words of John the Baptist in 1:29 and 1:34, is defined solely in terms of the cosmological tale, since it is the task of the Lamb of God to remove sin from the world.

The other major christological titles are also described with reference to the cosmological tale. For example, the Christ, sometimes translated in this gospel as Messiah (1:41), is described by the Samaritan woman as the one who is coming (4:25), a formula which appears to be short for "the one coming into the world" (cf. 11:27). In 4:42, the one whom the Samaritan woman dimly perceives to be the Christ is described by her compatriots as the Savior of the World, a title which derives directly from the soteriological function accorded to Jesus within the cosmological tale.[2]

"King of Israel" is the title given to Jesus by Nathanael (1:49). In Nathanael's testimony, the title bears some undefined relationship to the title "Son of God" as well as to Jesus' unexpected prior knowledge of Nathanael under the fig tree (1:48, 50). It surfaces again in the trial before Pilate, though the concept of kingship functions ironically in the Passion narrative as a whole.[3] In 18:36, Jesus declares that his kingship is not of this world, a declaration which

---

[1] This is virtually axiomatic in Johannine studies; see, for example, Schnack. 1.154–56.

[2] For a recent study of this title, see Craig R. Koester, "'The Savior of the World' (John 4:42)," *JBL* 109 (1990) 665–80.

[3] Paul D. Duke, *Irony in the Fourth Gospel* (Atlanta: John Knox, 1985) 126–37.

signals that the cosmological tale is drawing to a close: Jesus is now for all intents and purposes not in the world anymore; he is indeed King, who, though not of this world, has vanquished the ruler of this world and is therefore the one to whom all humankind owes allegiance.

The title "prophet" is given to Jesus by those who witness the feeding of the multitudes and on that basis believe that Jesus is the "prophet who is to come into the world" (6:14). Although it is clear that their faith is neither complete nor correct, the title of prophet nevertheless is not totally inappropriate as a christological description of Jesus.[4]

The most important christological titles in this gospel are "Son of Man" and "Son of God," or simply "Son." Unlike the other titles discussed above, which are used primarily by the narrator and/or other characters to refer to Jesus,[5] the titles referring to sonship appear most often on the lips of the Johannine Jesus, in apparent reference to himself.

These three titles are closely associated with one another, often appearing in the same context, as in 5:25–27:

> Verily truly, I tell you, the hour is coming, and is now here, when the dead will hear the voice of the *Son of God*, and those who hear will live. For just as the Father has life in himself, so has he granted the *Son* also to have life in himself; and he has given him authority to execute judgment, because he is the *Son of Man* (emphasis added).

In this passage, the three titles are related to one another and have the same referent—Jesus. They also allude to the cosmological tale by their connection to the God-given mission of Jesus (to give life and execute judgment) as it is described in that tale. Throughout the gospel, however, the titles "Son of God" and "Son of Man" appear in conjunction with two different sets of vocabulary, both of which have the cosmological tale as their frame of reference.

The "Son of God" title, often abbreviated to "Son,"[6] appears most often in the context of the language of sending and agency, with which the Fourth Gospel expresses the relationship between Jesus and God. The Johannine Jesus frequently refers to God as the "Father who sent me" (12:49; 14:24; 5:24, 37–38;

---

[4] Wayne A. Meeks, *The Prophet-King* (Leiden: Brill, 1967) passim; Adele Reinhartz, "Jesus as Prophet: Predictive Prolepses in the Fourth Gospel," *JSNT* 36 (1989) 3–16.

[5] The title "prophet" never appears on the lips of Jesus, while the title "Christ" is mentioned by Jesus only in 17:3, as part of the self-appellation "Jesus Christ." It is also implied in 4:26.

[6] For discussion of the relationships among the titles "Son of God," "Son of Man," and "Son," see Barnabas Lindars, "The Son of Man in Johannine Christology," *Christ and Spirit in the New Testament* (ed. B. Lindars and S. S. Smalley; Cambridge: Cambridge University Press, 1974) 43–60.

8:18, 42). That this formulation is rooted in the cosmological tale is clear, for example, in 7:28–29, in which Jesus declares to the people of Jerusalem, "I have not come on my own. But the one who sent me is true, and you do not know him. I know him, because I am from him, and he sent me."

The notion that Jesus is the Son of God sent by the Father into the world is the basis of the description of Jesus' mission according to the cosmological tale. Jesus has come in the Father's name (5:43), in order to do the Father's works, which testify that he was sent by the Father (5:17, 36). Furthermore, Jesus conveys the words and teachings of the Father, as he declares in 12:49: "...I have not spoken on my own, but the Father who sent me has himself given me a commandment about what to say and what to speak" (cf. also 7:16–17). Finally, Jesus does the will of the Father:

> ...I have come down from heaven, not to do my own will, but the will of him who sent me. And this is the will of him who sent me, that I should lose nothing of all that he has given me, but raise it up on the last day (6:38–39; cf. 17:6; 5:19–23).

In all of these acts, Jesus provides the means through which the believers—and the implied readers—can themselves know or see the Father. In 12:44–45, Jesus cries, "Whoever believes in me believes not in me but in him who sent me. And whoever sees me sees him who sent me." In 14:7, Jesus tells his disciples, "If you know me, you will know my Father also. From now on, you do know him and have seen him." The knowledge of the Father that is provided by the Son occupies much of Jesus' prayer in chapter 17. For example, in 17:3, Jesus declares eternal life to be the knowledge of "the only true God, and Jesus Christ whom you have sent." These comments echo the conclusion of the précis of the cosmological tale within the prologue (1:18), in which the narrator explains, "No one has ever seen God. It is God the only Son, who is close to the Father's heart, who has made him known."

The language of sending in itself implies movement of the one who is sent from one realm to another; this implication is reinforced by those passages in which this language is coupled with action verbs describing the activity of the one who is sent as "coming down from heaven" ($\kappa\alpha\tau\alpha\beta\acute{\epsilon}\beta\eta\kappa\alpha$ $\mathring{\alpha}\pi\grave{o}$ $\tauo\hat{v}$ $o\mathring{v}\rho\alpha\nuo\hat{v}$)(6:38). This is particularly clear in 8:42, in which Jesus tells the Jews, "If God were your Father, you would love me, for I came [$\mathring{\epsilon}\xi\hat{\eta}\lambda\thetao\nu$] from God and now I am here. I did not come [$\mathring{\epsilon}\lambda\acute{\eta}\lambda\upsilon\theta\alpha$] on my own, but he sent me." The cycle of movement is completed with those passages which speak of Jesus' return to the Father, such as 14:12, in which Jesus tells his disciples that he is going to the

Father (πορεύομαι), and 17:11 and 13, in which Jesus tells God, "Now I am coming [ἔρχομαι] to you..."

This brief survey of the relationship between the christological title "Son of God" and the cosmological tale situates the former firmly in the context of the latter. It is the language, concepts, and pattern of movement implied in the cosmological tale that provide the content for the title.

The title "Son of Man" is also connected firmly to language which implies movement through space, namely the language of ascent and descent. It appears first in 1:51, in which Jesus tells Nathanael, as well as the implied reader,[7] "Very truly, I tell you, you will see heaven opened and the angels of God ascending and descending upon the Son of Man." It is clear from this passage that the Son of Man is the ladder or means of connection between heaven and earth, while he himself remains anchored in both realms.

Elsewhere, it is the Son of Man himself who ascends and descends, as in 3:13, "No one has ascended [ἀναβέβηκεν] into heaven except the one who descended [καταβάς] from heaven, the Son of Man." The title is also embedded in the Bread of Life discourse, which emphasizes Jesus' descent from heaven. Although chapter 6 speaks of Jesus as the bread who came down [ὁ καταβαίνων] from heaven (e.g. 6:33), in the conclusion of Jesus' discourse, he responds to the complaints of his disciples by asking, "Does this offend you? Then what if you were to see the Son of Man ascending [ἀναβαίνοντα] to where he was before?" (6:62).

The vocabulary of ascent and descent clearly implies movement, but, in contrast to the language of coming and going which is prominent in the Son of God passages, it implies vertical spatial movement. This in turn implies a hierarchy and dualism of heaven and earth, according to which heaven has positive connotations while earth has negative ones. This dualism aligns "heaven" with "above" and "earth" with "world" (understood negatively) and "below" and is used by the implied author to distinguish "us" from "them," believers from non-believers. Hence the Johannine Jesus tells Nicodemus, "If I have told you about earthly things and you do not believe, how can you believe if I tell you about heavenly things? No one has ascended into heaven except the one who descended from heaven, the Son of Man" (3:12–13). The dualism is continued in 3:31: "The one who comes from above [ἐπάνω] is above all; the one who is of the earth [ἐκ τῆς γῆς] belongs to the earth and speaks about earthly things. The one who comes from heaven is above all."

---

[7] Significant here is the use of the second person plural pronoun, although in the narrative context Jesus explicitly addresses an individual.

Using strong language, he accuses the Jews, "You are from below [ἐκ τῶν κάτω], I am from above [ἐκ τῶν ἄνω]; you are of this world, I am not of this world" (8:23). This language becomes even more pointed in 8:44: "You are from your father the Devil, and you choose to do your Father's desires." This serves to contrast the Jews with Jesus, who is from his Father God, whose desires he performs. Hence the Son of Man title, in its connection with the language of ascent and descent, evokes the opposition that Jesus, as the Word of God, faced in the world, which is the central conflict of the cosmological tale as told in the prologue and throughout the gospel narrative.

This brief survey of the major christological titles applied to Jesus in the Gospel of John suggests that all are linked in one way or another to the vocabulary and major stages of the cosmological tale. The most significant of these titles is the Son of God, through which Jesus' relationship with God is described.

"I am": ἐγώ εἰμί. The titles, prominent as they are, are not the only vehicles for Johannine christology. Among the many other expressions of christology is the ἐγώ εἰμί formulation, which Jesus uses either absolutely, as in 8:58,[8] or with a completion, as in 14:6.[9] A brief examination of four of the ἐγώ εἰμί passages will indicate that they too are rooted in the cosmological tale.

In 4:26, Jesus uses the formulation absolutely, declaring to the Samaritan woman, "I am he, the one who is speaking to you." In this case, the completion "the Messiah" is implied, since Jesus' words are in response to the woman's comment, "I know that Messiah is coming [ἔρχεται] (who is called Christ). When he comes [ἔλθῃ], he will proclaim all things to us" (4:25). The presence of the words "comes" and "is coming" signal the cosmological tale.

Verse 8:58 contains the absolute use of the ἐγώ εἰμί formulation. In the conclusion of Jesus' confrontation with the Jews, he declares, "Very truly, I tell you, before Abraham was, I am." This is usually read as a reference to Jesus' pre-existence, the first stage of the cosmological tale as described in the prologue.

In 11:25, Jesus tells Martha, "I am the resurrection and the life. Those who believe in me will never die." This connection between faith and eternal life echoes the language of many other passages in which a similar link is made using the language of the cosmological tale, as in 5:24: "Very truly I tell you, anyone who hears my word and believes him who sent me has eternal life, and does not come under judgment, but has passed from death to life."

---

8 E.g., 8:24, 28; 13:19. For discussion of the ἐγώ εἰμί formula, see AB 1.533–38.
9 E.g., 6:35, 51; 8:21; 9:5; 10:7, 9, 11, 14; 11:25; 14:6; 15:1, 5. See also 6:20 and 18:5, in which a predicate is implied.

The final example is 14:6, "I am the way, and the truth, and the life. No one comes to the Father except through me." This expresses the claim that we have already encountered in our discussion of the Son of God passages, namely that one of the principal purposes of Jesus' activity in the world is to make the Father known and to provide a means through which the believer can have some knowledge of, and access to, the Father.

The above discussion shows the point of contact between various christological formulations and the cosmological tale. Not only do these formulations all include some direct reference to the plot and vocabulary of the cosmological tale, but their meaning and significance for the reader are most easily understood within the context of that tale. This suggests that the cosmological tale does indeed function as a primary vehicle for conveying the christological understanding of the implied author to the implied reader.

THE SELF-UNDERSTANDING OF THE IMPLIED READER

As 20:30–31 and numerous other passages make clear, an intellectual understanding of Jesus' christological identity is not sufficient. What is important is the reader's response to and acceptance of Jesus' identity as Messiah. The ideal response to Jesus as the Christ is referred to throughout the gospel by such terms as receiving (1:12), following (1:43), and believing (20:31). Furthermore, different responses to Jesus, both negative and positive, are portrayed by the characters in the gospel. Perhaps the strongest example of a negative response is the rejection of Jesus on the part of the Jews or the Jewish establishment,[10] who attempt to stone him (8:59) and are ultimately responsible, according to the implied author, for his death (11:45–53; 18:13).

On the other hand, varying degrees and stages of faith are portrayed, such as the inadequate faith of those who, after the cleansing of the temple, "believed in his name because they saw the signs that he was doing" (2:23); the developing but secret faith of Nicodemus (3:1–15; 7:50; 19:39);[11] the signs-faith of the Roman official (4:48, 53); culminating in the profound confessions of faith of

---

[10] For discussion of the referent of the term "Jews" in this gospel, see Carson, *Fourth Gospel*, 131–34.

[11] Marinus de Jonge ("Nicodemus and Jesus: Some Observations on Misunderstanding and Understanding in the Fourth Gospel," *Jesus*, 29–47), suggests that Nicodemus is an example of a crypto-Christian, a view which is rejected by Brown (*Community*, 72, note 128). See also Sarah J. Tanzer, "Salvation is for the Jews: Secret Christian Jews in the Gospel of John," *The Future of Early Christianity: Essays in Honor of Helmut Koester* (ed. Birger Pearson; Minneapolis: Fortress, 1991) 291–95. A different analysis is proposed by Jouette M. Bassler ("Mixed Signals: Nicodemus in the Fourth Gospel," *JBL* 108 [1989] 635–46), who focuses on Nicodemus as an ambiguous and marginal character in the gospel.

Martha (11:27)[12] and Thomas (20:28). These examples are amplified by the many references to faith in the discourse portions of the gospel, which are unanimous in linking faith with the knowledge of and belief in the elements of the cosmological tale. For example, 3:16 describes God's love for the world, which was so strong that he gave his only Son in order that "everyone who believes in him should not perish but have eternal life." Here the emphasis is on God's purpose in sending his Son into the world, which will be saved through its belief in the Son (3:17). This idea is reiterated in 3:18: "Those who believe in him are not condemned; but those who do not believe are condemned already, because they have not believed in the name of the only Son of God." Therefore being saved is conditional on belief; condemnation, which is the situation of the world in the absence of Jesus, is for those who do not believe and therefore continue to live as though the Son of God had not been sent into the world.

The content of faith therefore appears to be knowledge of and belief in Jesus as described in the cosmological tale. But the implied reader is required not only to give intellectual assent to a set of specific theological propositions, but also to re-orient his or her perspective on salvation, life, death, and the world in the light of the cosmological tale. To do this, implied readers must situate themselves within the gospel in such a way that they perceive themselves to be both the addressees and the subjects of the gospel.

What allows and indeed encourages readers to do this is the way in which the cosmological tale redefines the temporal and spatial horizons of the historical and ecclesiological tales. As we have already remarked, these tales are each assigned to a specific time and place. The historical tale belongs to early first-century Palestine, the ecclesiological tale to a community in the late first-century Diaspora.[13] In contrast, the cosmological tale is universal in location and has eternity as its time frame. As such, it constitutes the larger temporal and spatial framework within which the historical and ecclesiological tales are played out.

This point is made apparent to the reader by the presence of the prologue. By introducing the narrative with an account of the beginning of the cosmological tale, the narrator invites the reader to understand the historical tale as only one stage, albeit a crucial one, in the "life" of Jesus the Word and his relationship with the world. The fact that the temporal framework of the cosmological tale will be closed only at the future return of Christ allows the

---

12 Adele Reinhartz, "From Narrative to History: The Resurrection of Martha and Mary," *Women Like This: New Perspectives on Jewish Women in the Greco-Roman World* (ed. Amy-Jill Levine; SBLEJL 1; Atlanta: Scholars Press, 1991) 161–84.
13 See AB 1.ciii–iv.

implied reader, likely a member of the Johannine community, to place the post–Easter ecclesiological tale within this eternal temporal framework as well.

Indeed, the implied reader is explicitly encouraged to do this by the passages in the gospel which speak of the role and experience of the disciples in the world in the time between Jesus' departure to the Father, which is the conclusion of the gospel narrative, and his later return to the world, the *parousia,* which is the conclusion of the cosmological tale. Important in this regard are the references to the paraclete, whom Jesus will send after his departure to continue his work in the world (14:26; 15:26; 16:7–11). Also relevant are references to those who come to faith through the words and activities of Jesus' disciples. This is alluded to in 13:20, in which Jesus tells the disciples, "Very truly, I tell you, whoever receives one whom I send receives me; and whoever receives me receives him who sent me." This theme is expressed more clearly in 17:20, in which Jesus speaks to God on behalf of the disciples and "those who will believe in me through their word...," and in 20:29, in which Jesus gently chides Thomas, "Have you believed because you have seen me? Blessed are those who have not seen and yet have come to believe."

In addition to providing for the continuation of the mission, these passages provide entrance to what we have termed the sub-tale of the gospel, namely, the ecclesiological tale. The implied readers, as members of the Johannine community, can read themselves into the gospel by realizing that the historical tale can be read "representationally" to provide insight into the history and experience of the Johannine community. It also legitimates the authority claims of that community by suggesting that it is the recipient of the spirit (20:22) and in possession of the paraclete who continues the work of divine revelation. At the same time that the gospel addresses the Johannine community through the ecclesiological tale, it also provides a broader temporal framework for that tale as well. Just as the historical tale is only one stage in the history of Jesus' relationship with the world, so also is the ecclesiological tale. Because the *parousia* which will bring the cosmological tale to its proper conclusion has not yet occurred, real readers—of all eras—are also invited to place their own individual tales within the context of the cosmological tale.

The universal spatial framework of the cosmological tale operates in a similar fashion. In the first place, the historical tale is understood as taking place only in one specific location in the world, namely, Palestine, with episodes set in Galilee, Samaria and Judea. This location, however, is likely not identical with that of the implied readers.[14] By providing a broader spatial setting, the cosmological tale allows the implied readers—whose trials and tribulations are

---

[14] On the provenance of the Johannine community, see page 3 above.

alluded to in the ecclesiological tale—to locate themselves in the Fourth Gospel, despite the fact they themselves do not hail from Palestine. The same will be true of those real readers who identify with the implied reader. Though only a relatively small group of Jews in Galilee and Judea actually saw the historical Jesus, the paraclete is sent to the world as a whole, the disciples are sent out into the world, and Christ will return to the world. Just as the post-ascension believers are not excluded temporally from the hopes of salvation, neither are they excluded by virtue of their location in the world.

In conclusion, the cosmological tale provides the temporal and spatial framework for the historical and ecclesiological tales, and through its open-ended conclusion allows room for the implied reader in the history of salvation. In doing so, the tale encourages real readers to locate themselves within its temporal and spatial framework, just as the characters of the historical tale and the implied readers within the ecclesiological tale do. It is therefore by universalizing the specific temporal and spatial boundaries of the historical and ecclesiological tales that the cosmological tale allows and encourages readers to situate themselves within the gospel and to see themselves as its addressees. In reading themselves into the time and place of the cosmological tale, readers must confront the Johannine understanding of the "world" into which Jesus came, in which the readers also find themselves. It is in the process of such confrontation that the implied readers are given the opportunity to rethink their self-understanding and their stance towards both the Word and the world.

The World

We have thus far considered the "world" primarily as a spatial entity, as the location into which Jesus enters, in which he is active, and from which he departs. As such it has the effect that we have already noted, namely, that of universalizing the scope of Jesus' mission. But it is readily apparent that the term "world" is not merely a spatial term. It is also used metaphorically to refer to the human inhabitants of the world. In many passages, the reference is not specific, and so could be understood universally, as, for example, in 3:17: "Indeed, God did not send the Son into the world to condemn the world, but in order that the world might be saved through him."[15] In other passages, however, the "world" seems to refer specifically to the Jews among whom Jesus sojourned and acted. For example, the narrator declares in 1:10: "He was in the world, and the world came into being through him; yet the world did not know him." The general

---

[15] See also 4:42; 6:14; 6:33; 8:12; 8:26; 12:47.

definition of world implied in this verse is immediately narrowed to a specific location and community by the verse which follows: "He came to what was his own [εἰς τά ἴδια],[16] and his own people did not accept him" (1:11). By drawing on later passages in which those who reject Jesus are clearly the Jews, the referent for "world" here can be identified as the Jews. This is apparent also in 7:4, in which Jesus' brothers attempt to persuade Jesus to come up to Jerusalem for the Feast of Tabernacles by arguing: "...no man who wants to be widely known acts in secret. If you do these things, show yourself to the world."

These latter passages set up a situation in which the implied reader, in order to identify with the perspective of the implied author, must resist identifying with the world that is opposing Jesus' message. This need is reinforced by the many passages in which the world, though not identified specifically as the unbelieving Jews, is described in negative terms.

This is implied in the first place by passages which indicate the necessity not only for Jesus but for his followers to separate themselves from the world. The disciples have been given to Jesus by God from, or out of, the world (17:6); they are "in the world" (17:11), but not of the world (17:14, 16; cf. 15:19). Jesus enters the world (1:9; 3:17; 6:14; 9:39; 10:36; 12:47) in order to save its inhabitants (3:17; 4:42; 12:47),[17] implying that the world apart from Jesus is in need of salvation. In saving the world, he will eventually lead those inhabitants who believe in him out of the world to his Father's house (14:2–3). In these passages, therefore, the image of the world is a negative one, representing a situation from which the believers must be removed in order to attain "life" or salvation.[18]

This idea is made more explicit by the passages which use the images of light and darkness. The constant reference to Jesus as the light of the world implies that without him, the world is in darkness. For example, in 3:19 the reader is told that "the light has come into the world, and people loved darkness rather than light because their deeds were evil." In 8:12, Jesus tells his audience, "I am the light of the world. Whoever follows me will never walk in darkness, but will have the light of life" (cf. also 9:5; 11:9; 12:46). A related characteristic

---

[16] This was translated by the old RSV as "his own home."

[17] In some instances, the world is a physical, or spatial category, in others, it refers to the human inhabitants of the physical world. Cf. 1:10, where both meanings are present, and discussion on pages 75-80 below.

[18] A similar conclusion is drawn by D. A. Carson (*Divine Sovereignty and Human Responsibility* [Atlanta: John Knox, 1981] 164), who argues that there are in fact no positive references to the world in this gospel. He understands all verses which appear to be positive as refering to God and his salvific purposes. Even some of the apparently neutral instances of the term pave the way for the crime of unbelief and "negative universalism," underscoring the Johannine conviction that all sin before the coming of Christ.

is the association of the world and sin. This is made explicit in 1:29, in which John the Baptist refers to Jesus as the "Lamb of God, who takes away the sin of the world." While this passage has been interpreted in many different ways,[19] it identifies sin as a condition of the world into which Jesus came.

These passages set up an antithetical relationship between being in the world (a negative condition) and not being in the world (a positive condition.) This is expressed explicitly in 8:23, in which Jesus tells the Jews, "You are from below, I am from above; you are of this world, I am not of this world." That the world, the realm of physical life, is antithetical to spiritual life, is indicated in 12:25: "Those who love their life lose it, and those who hate their life in this world will keep it for eternal life." Furthermore, the world cannot receive the spirit of truth (14:17); it hates Jesus and his disciples because they are not of the world (7:7; 17:14).

These passages underscore a basic assumption of the cosmological tale, namely that it is necessary for believers to leave behind the darkness and sin of this world in order to be saved. Since being saved is described as having "life in his name" (20:31) and as passing from death to life (5:24), it would appear that not believing, not following Jesus, is a condition akin to death. Those remaining in the darkness of the world as it was before Jesus' entry, and as it remains now apart from faith in him, suffer condemnation, the wrath of God, and ultimately, "eternal death." As Jesus tells the Jews in 8:21, 24: "I am going away, and you will search for me, but you will die in your sin. Where I am going, you cannot come....I told you that you would die in your sins, for you will die in your sins unless you believe that I am he." Conversely, "whoever keeps my word will never see death" (8:51).

The cosmological tale therefore not only redefines "life" but also the concept of "death." Death is not only the physical condition which awaits all human beings at the end of their lives, but also, and more importantly, it characterizes the spiritual condition of humankind apart from Christ's saving power. Those who are spiritually dead have no hope of escaping eternal condemnation, while those who are spiritually alive in the present, having acknowledged Christ as savior, will not be affected by their physical deaths, but will enjoy the resurrection of life.

In this redefined sense, death is characteristic of the world of darkness which opposes Jesus' message. Jesus' entry into the world, however, provides the

---

[19] See AB 1.58–63, for a discussion of the range of interpretations given to 1:29. It is interesting to note that 1:29 also uses pastoral language to refer to Jesus, though here he is lamb rather than shepherd.

opportunity for resurrection for the "living dead" inhabiting the world of darkness upon Jesus' arrival. This is implied in 5:24, in which Jesus says to the Jews: "Very truly, I tell you, anyone who hears my word and believes him who sent me has eternal life; and does not come under judgment, but has passed from death to life." The next verse apparently identifies those who have lived in the world without Christ as the dead who are now given life: "Very truly, I tell you, the hour is coming, and is now here, when the dead will hear the voice of the Son of God, and those who hear will live...." Verses 5:28–29, however, seem to redefine these νεκροί as the physically dead whom Jesus will raise from the tomb, as he does his friend Lazarus (11:43–44):

> Do not be astonished at this; for the hour is coming when all who are in their graves will hear his voice and come out—those who have done good, to the resurrection of life, and those who have done evil, to the resurrection of condemnation.

This progression of thought in 5:24–29 in effect blurs the distinction between those who are physically dead and waiting in their tombs, and those who are physically alive but are, or have been, spiritually dead due to the absence of Jesus from the world. The obscuring of the differences and boundaries between these two concepts, however, serves a definite purpose, namely to associate life in this world apart from Jesus with death in such a way as to underscore the vital necessity of faith. In doing so, the implied author also muddies the boundaries between realized and future eschatology.[20]

This brief survey indicates that the cosmological tale serves to broaden the temporal and spatial framework of the gospel to include the implied readers and potentially the real readers, wherever and whenever they might live. Furthermore, by defining the κόσμος into which Jesus came as the world of sin, darkness, and death, the cosmological tale is a powerful tool for conveying the perspective of the implied author. Ideally the implied reader, and the real reader as well, in the reading of the gospel will come to see life apart from Jesus as death in the most profound spiritual sense, thereby adopting the point of view of the implied author.[21]

---

[20] See the interesting discussion of this passage in J. G. van der Watt, "A New Look at John 5:25–29 in the Light of the Use of the Term 'Eternal Life' in the Gospel according to John," *Neot* 19 (1985) 71–86.

[21] This is the case even if the gospel is directed towards Christian members of the Johannine community.

INTERPRETIVE KEY

The cosmological tale guides the readers of the gospel to a particular understanding not only of Jesus and of themselves, but also of the gospel narrative itself. From the prologue through to the Passion, the Johannine Jesus and the narrator provide clues to the meaning which readers should assign to, or derive from, the specific events which comprise the historical tale. The narrator does this by describing the responses of particular characters to events which they witnessed; the Johannine Jesus does so in the discourses which the implied author has attached to some of the signs-narratives.[22] The role of the cosmological tale in providing the correct, that is, the implied author's, interpretation of the historical tale is readily apparent in a brief survey of the narrative and discourse portions of the gospel.

Narrative. Instructions regarding the proper interpretation of the signs-narratives, which provide the backbone of the gospel narrative as a whole, are to be found both in the narrator's comments as well as in comments attributed to the Johannine Jesus. For example, the reader is clearly instructed to view Jesus' actions in turning water into wine at the Cana wedding not simply as an inexpensive way of alleviating social embarrassment but as the manifestation of his glory (2:11). The healing of the centurion's son is not only evidence of Jesus' healing powers but provides an example of people who believe without themselves seeing the full result of Jesus' activity.[23] The healing of the lame man is connected with Jesus' ability to remove sin from the world (5:14) and provides the occasion for the theological discourse in which Jesus proclaims his identity as the Son of God. The multiplication of loaves and fishes does not merely provide refreshment for a hungry crowd but points to Jesus' identity as the bread of eternal life "which came down from heaven" (6:58). The healing of the blind man is important not because a man's lifelong disability has been corrected but because it reveals Jesus' identity as the light of the world (9:5). Finally, the raising of Lazarus not only demonstrates that Jesus' life-giving powers extend beyond the grave, but also states clearly that it is because of the Father that Jesus has those powers at all, thereby demonstrating the glory of God (11:40). The final narrative portion, the crucifixion of Jesus, is also not what it seems to be— the ignominious death of a troublemaking hero—but an essential element of

---

[22] This is the basis of C. H. Dodd's analysis of the narrative structure of the gospel. See Dodd, 308 and passim.

[23] For example, the nobleman in 4:46–54 believes without seeing his child healed. See page 103 below.

Jesus' glorification (17:1), by which he will draw all people to himself (12:32), and after which he will ascend to where he had come from (20:17).

The clues which the implied author provides regarding the meaning and significance of the signs-narratives are not abstract christological tenets but have their place in the coherent narrative structure of the cosmological tale. Furthermore, the structure of the cosmological tale mirrors the structure of the historical tale. Both begin with Jesus' entry into the physical and temporal setting; they continue by describing Jesus' activities within that setting; when Jesus begins to prepare himself, his disciples, and his readers for his death on the cross, he also prepares them for his return to the Father. It may therefore be said that the cosmological tale, as the meta-tale, is the frame of reference which provides the explicit interpretive key for the events of the historical tale.[24]

Discourse. In his discourses, the Johannine Jesus speaks directly to his audience in the gospel as well as to the implied readers concerning his identity and mission. Although the language in which he does so can be difficult and elusive,[25] and the theological claims which that language implies can be complex and at times contradictory,[26] the framework into which much of the language and theology fits is clearly the cosmological tale. For example, Jesus' discussion with Nicodemus (3:1ff.) focuses on the redeemer who has descended from heaven and speaks of heavenly things to those who can hear him, and will ascend again (3:13–15). Chapter 5:10–47 discusses the relationship between the Son and the Father who sent him, and the importance of that relationship for those who believe. Chapter 6:22–71, the Bread of Life discourse, explores similar themes against the background of the Exodus event during which God provided manna to ensure the Israelites' survival. The debate in chapter 7 over Jesus' true identity makes ironic use of some of the central elements of the cosmological tale, such as Jesus' origins and ultimate destination. Jesus concludes his heated discussion with the Jews in chapter 8 by referring to his own pre-existence, a statement for which the Jews attempt to stone him. In his conversation with the man born blind (9:39), Jesus declares judgment to be the purpose for which he came into the world. Verses 10:22–39 and 11:41–42 return to the theme of the relationship between the Father and the Son, while 12:27–50 emphasizes the purpose for which Jesus was sent into the world and the crucial decision that must be made by the individual in response to Jesus' coming. The Farewell

---

[24] This of course does not rule out the possibility of other interpretations.

[25] Throughout the gospel, Jesus' language is misunderstood by the characters he addresses in the narrative (e.g. Nicodemus, in chapter 3, and the Jews in chapters 6 and 8).

[26] The most difficult of these contradictions concerns eschatology, as in 5:24–29, which uses the language of both present and future eschatology.

Discourses, chapters 13–17, continue the Johannine Jesus' exploration of these topics and many others related to the cosmological tale, including the preparations for Jesus' departure (13:21–30), the coming of the paraclete (14:26; 15:26; 16:7–11), and the role of the disciples in the world after Jesus' departure (ch. 17; 20:21).

IRONY

The above observations demonstrate that the cosmological tale is the meta-tale within the gospel, that is, the overall frame which gives meaning to the narrative, discourse, theology, and metaphors of the gospel, at least from the perspective of the implied author. One illustration of how the cosmological tale functions as meta-tale may be found in the extensive use of irony.[27] Numerous studies have discussed the role of irony in the gospel.[28] Our discussion will focus on irony as one way in which the implied reader is to use the cosmological tale to understand what the characters in the gospel cannot.

In looking at the passages which speak clearly of the cosmological tale, it is apparent that many of them are found in the words of the narrator rather than on the lips of the Johannine Jesus or any other character in this gospel. This is true, for example, of such key passages as 1:1–18, 3:16–21, and 3:31–36.[29] This indicates that even the disciples, who were present during almost all of the signs and discourses of Jesus,[30] did not have a full understanding of the cosmological tale until the conclusion of the farewell discourses. In 16:25, 28, Jesus tells his disciples:

> I have said these things to you in figures of speech. The hour is coming when I will no longer speak to you in figures, but will tell you plainly of the Father...I came from the Father and have come into the world; again, I am leaving the world and am going to the Father.

Their response is one of relief:

---

27 Culpepper, 152.

28 See Duke, *Irony*; Gail R. O'Day, *Revelation in the Fourth Gospel* (Philadelphia: Fortress, 1986); and S. D. Moore, "Rifts in (a reading of) the fourth gospel, or: Does Johannine irony still collapse on a reading that draws attention to itself?" *Neot* 23 (1989) 5–17.

29 This is the view of many scholars, including R. G. Lightfoot (*St. John's Gospel* [London: Oxford University Press, 1956] 118, 120), though it is rejected by Brown, AB 1.149.

30 Virtually the only incident to which the disciples were not witness is Jesus' encounter with the Samaritan woman, 4:1–44. Apparently in this section the implied author was more concerned to demonstrate Jesus' willingness to remain alone with a Samaritan woman (4:27) than to provide a witness for the scene.

Yes, now you are speaking plainly, not in any figure of speech! Now we know that you know all things, and do not need to have anyone to question you; by this we believe that you came from God. (16:29–30)

This special knowledge to which the reader but not the characters are privy is essential to irony as communication between implied author and implied reader. If the cosmological tale is the interpretive key to Johannine narrative and theology, and if it is fully known to the characters only at the conclusion of the gospel (if then), it may be seen as part of the special knowledge which the implied author conveys to the implied readers in order that they might understand the ironic passages within the gospel.

To illustrate this point, it will be useful to look at the series of ironic dialogues in chapter 7, in which, despite his words to the contrary (7:8), the Johannine Jesus goes up to Jerusalem during the Feast of Tabernacles. Once in Jerusalem, he encounters crowds who are busily debating whether or not he fulfills the criteria of the Messiah. In 7:27, the people declare that "we know where this man is from; but when the Messiah [Christ] appears, no one will know where he is from." In the context of the historical tale, this would seem to be a reference to Jesus' Galilean origins. Jesus' response is to counter with an allusion to his origins as described in the cosmological tale:

You know me, and you know where I come from. I have not come on my own. But the one who sent me is true, and you do not know him. I know him, because I am from him, and he sent me. (7:28)

It is not surprising that the crowd, which has not read the prologue or 3:16–19, does not understand this, but for the readers this message is consistent with the other passages which describe Jesus' origins (e.g. 8:42).

A second example in this chapter is found in 7:33–34. In these verses, Jesus declares: "I will be with you a little longer, and then I am going to him who sent me; you will search for me, but you will not find me; where I am, you cannot come." In making sense of this statement, the reader is able to rely on what he or she knows from earlier readings of the gospel, namely that Jesus will shortly depart and return to the Father to complete this phase of the cosmological tale. The Jews, however, misunderstand completely and wonder, "Does he intend to go to the Dispersion among the Greeks and teach the Greeks?" (7:35). This response not only exhibits Jewish misunderstanding of Jesus, which is a prevalent theme in this gospel,[31] but provides the occasion for a further irony which is not spelled out. By going to the Father, Jesus allows the continuation of his mission by means of the paraclete and the disciples whom he has sent into the world. As the readers, whether members of the Johannine community or not, know, this continuation resulted in the preaching of the message to the Greeks in the dispersion. This development would have been apparent to the implied reader not only from hints in the gospel (10:16; 12:24), but also from first-hand knowledge of the inclusion of Gentiles in the Christian community after the death of Jesus.[32]

A third example of irony is found in the people's query in 7:41–42: "Surely the Messiah [Christ] does not come from Galilee, does he? Has not the scripture said that the Messiah [Christ] is descended from David and comes from Bethlehem, the village where David lived?" Although Raymond E. Brown has suggested that the reader is meant to supply extrinsic knowledge of Jesus' birth in Bethlehem,[33] it may be argued that the main point here is to reiterate the message of 7:28–29, that Jesus' true origins are with the Father; the geographical point at which he happened to enter this world is irrelevant to his true identity as the Christ and Son of God.

CONCLUSION

These examples indicate that the reader would have drawn on the cosmological tale in order to understand what the characters in the gospel have failed to do. In the case of the ironic passages in chapter 7, as well as in other examples of misunderstanding between Jesus and various individuals and groups in other chapters, the communication between implied author and implied reader is relatively easy to decipher. But the usefulness of the cosmological tale as a frame of reference in these cases raises the interesting methodological possibility that the cosmological tale might prove helpful in deciphering other, more obscure, cases of misunderstanding.

A prime example on which to test out this possibility is the *paroimia* of the shepherd and the sheep in John 10:1–5. The implied, and real, readers of this passage are directly challenged by the narrator's comment in 10:6, that Jesus' audience within the narrative failed to understand what he was saying to them. After looking at how New Testament exegetes have risen to this challenge, we

---

[31] See Culpepper, 152–65, and literature cited there.
[32] Brown (*Community*, 55–58) sees "clear signs of a Gentile component among the recipients of the Gospel."
[33] AB 1.330.

will examine carefully how the cosmological tale might act as the interpretive key which the readers, unlike the characters within the narrative, can use to unlock its meaning.

3

SCHOLARLY READINGS OF JOHN 10:1–5

We begin our study of 10:1–5 by describing the *paroimia* in its narrative context in the Fourth Gospel and then examining the ways in which the passage has been read by a specific group of real readers, namely, New Testament scholars.

JOHN 10:1–5

(1) Very truly, I tell you, anyone who does not enter the sheepfold by the door but climbs in by another way is a thief and a bandit. (2) The one who enters by the gate [or door: *thura*] is the shepherd of the sheep. (3) The gatekeeper opens the gate for him, and the sheep hear his voice. He calls his own sheep by name and leads them out. (4) When he has brought out all his own, he goes ahead of them, and the sheep follow him because they know his voice. (5) They will not follow a stranger, but they will run from him because they do not know the voice of strangers.

The structure and principal elements of the passage are relatively easy to identify. The passage begins with a contrast between the shepherd and the thief. The latter climbs into the sheepfold by stealth (10:1). In contrast, the shepherd enters by the gate, which is opened to him by the gatekeeper (10:2–3a). Verses 3b–4 describe the relationship between the shepherd and his sheep: they hear his voice and follow him; he calls them by name, leads them out of the fold, and goes before them. Verse 5 returns to the contrast begun in verse 1 by referring to the stranger whom the sheep do not heed because they do not know his voice. Therefore the two main themes of the *paroimia* are the contrast between the shepherd and the forces which oppose him—thief, bandit, stranger—and the confidential, exclusive relationship between the shepherd and the sheep.

The structure of the passage can therefore be mapped out in the following way:

A. Contrast between shepherd and thief/bandit regarding entry into the fold (10:1–2)
B. The shepherd's activity in the fold (10:3)
C. Contrast between shepherd and stranger regarding leading the sheep out of the fold (10:4–5).

The description of the shepherd's activity in the fold, which focuses on his relationship to the sheep, is framed by references to the contrast between shepherd and opponent, that is, the thief/bandit of 10:1 and the stranger of 10:5.[1] This would imply that functionally, the thief and the stranger play the same role in the *paroimia*.[2]

The *paroimia* is structured around several elements, which are described in relationship with one another. The main elements are the three characters—the shepherd, the sheep, the opponent—and the place within which they interact— the sheepfold. The elements of the gate and the gatekeeper do not function independently but are related to that of the sheepfold, serving to control entry into the fold by legitimating the shepherd's identity and his rightful access to the sheep.

JOHN 10:6

That 10:1–5 constitute a discrete unit is indicated not only by the *inclusio* in verses 1 and 5, but also by the narrator's comment in 10:6: "Jesus used this figure of speech [ἡ παροιμία] with them, but they did not understand what he was saying to them." With these words, the implied author, by means of the narrator's voice, challenges the implied reader to succeed where Jesus' audience has failed.[3]

John 10:6 itself provides a starting point for the reader keen on rising to the challenge. First, 10:6 labels the preceding five verses as a *paroimia*, or figurative discourse, that is, as a passage which should not be taken at face value but rather requires interpretation. Second, it works together with 10:7a to act as a bridge between 10:1–5 and 7–18. It therefore signals to the reader that the latter

---

[1] See Odo Kiefer, *Die Hirtenrede* (Stuttgart: Verlag Katholisches Bibelwerk, 1967) 12.

[2] This is assumed by most scholars. See, for example, Quasten, 7.

[3] As noted in the previous chapter, other passages in the gospel serve a similar function, including the examples of irony and misunderstanding. See D. A. Carson, "Understanding and Misunderstanding in the Fourth Gospel," *TynBul* 33 (1982) 59–91.

section, which continues the pastoral imagery of the former, is not formally a part of the *paroimia*; rather, it is in some sense an explication or extension thereof. Third, 10:6 implies a connection between the preceding chapter and 10:1–5. This connection is indicated not only by the juxtaposition of chapters 9 and 10, but also by the fact that no new narrative setting or audience is specified in 10:6 for Jesus' words in 10:1–5.[4] The setting of chapter 9, which would appear to be the temple at the Feast of Tabernacles,[5] and the audience, namely, the Pharisees (cf. 9:40), by implication extend to the *paroimia* too.[6]

In this way, the narrator's comment in 10:6 points to the issues of genre and context as factors to be taken into special consideration in the interpretation of the passage. We shall now consider how some more recent real readers have gone about using this intratextual information.[7]

GENRE OF 10:1–5

The narrator in 10:6 labels the passage a *paroimia*. The word *paroimia* is translated in most lexicons as a figure of speech, a proverb, or a saying.[8] Aside from its three occurrences in the Fourth Gospel (10:6; 16:25, 29), the term is present in the New Testament only in 2 Peter 2:22. In the latter, it refers simply

---

[4] The nearest available antecedent for the pronoun "they" in 10:6, describing Jesus' uncomprehending audience, is the Pharisees in 9:40.

[5] AB 1.376.

[6] The formula "very truly, I tell you" does not generally begin a new discourse in the gospel, but is used to emphasize an important point, or alter the direction of discussion. By the time they read John 10, the implied readers have encountered this formula numerous times and would not have seen it as necessarily beginning a new section. What is perhaps confusing about this to modern readers is the abrupt change in content of the passage as well as the fact that 10:1 begins a new chapter. Ancient readers, not having chapter divisions, would not have used the chapter break as information in their interpretation of the passage, and hence would have attached it to the last-named temporal and physical setting, namely the temple at the Feast of Tabernacles. See Dodd, 358, and Godet, 380.

[7] It must be noted that few scholarly treatments deal explicitly or at length with the issue of reader-reception, for the excellent reason that most of them were written before this issue became a concern for students of New Testament narrative. Rather, most Johannine exegetes approach the task of interpreting the passage as historical-critics. Implicit in their approach is the assumption that the meaning which they derive from this text is the meaning intended by its author and/or speaker, in this case Jesus and/or the Fourth Evangelist. That there is some identity between this intended meaning and the meaning which the original audience would have assigned to the passage is implied on the basis of the assumption that the speaker/writer would have intended his meaning to be understood by his audience. To some extent, these assumptions are inherent in the very task of exegesis, and this is as true for literary or reader-oriented approaches to the gospel as for historical-critical ones.

[8] S.v. παροιμία, LSJ and BAGD. For a preliminary study, see Kim E. Dewey, "*Paroimia* in the Gospel of John," *Semeia* 17 (1980) 81–100.

to a well-known proverb or saying.[9] In John 16, however, speaking in ἐν
παροιμίαις is specifically contrasted to speaking παρρησία, i.e., plainly. This
implies that the *paroimia* is a way of saying figuratively what could also be
expressed plainly. Built into the Johannine usage of this term, therefore, are,
first, the notion of a correspondence between the plain and figurative modes of
discourse, and second, the need for interpretation. The latter involves the
deciphering of the figurative code by determining to what "plain" meaning the
figurative language was meant to correspond and what message it was intended
to convey. Hence a good working definition of *paroimia* would be that of James
Martin, who defines it as a symbolic saying which requires interpretation.[10]

Many scholars, however, are not content with a general definition but seek
to define *paroimia* as a specific genre found in other early Christian texts. The
issue comes down to whether the *paroimia* is a parable, an allegory, both, or
neither. The definition of the genre of 10:1–5 to a great extent determines how a
scholar understands the source and allusions of the pastoral imagery, as well as
the methodology used in interpreting the passage and the specific meaning
which he or she assigns to it.

The tendency among older scholars, from the patristic period to the early
twentieth century, was to read the *paroimia* as an allegory, which they generally
understood as a figurative saying the structure and main elements of which were
determined by the "plain" meaning which it was meant to convey.[11] The key to
interpreting the passage, according to this view, was therefore to determine the
referents of each of its elements.

A good example of this approach is found in F. Godet's commentary from
1892. Godet argues that the picture drawn in 10:1–5

> ...deserves rather to be called an allegory than a parable. In the
> parable, the thought is clothed in a form which, to a certain extent, has
> a meaning independent of its moral application; in the allegory, the
> application is directly felt in each feature of the picture, and there is
> not time for the image to take a form independent of the thought.[12]

---

[9] See Bo Reicke, *The Epistles of James, Peter and Jude* (AB 37; New York: Doubleday, 1964)
172.

[10] James P. Martin, "John 10:1–10," *Int* 32 (1978) 171–75.

[11] The definitions of and relationship between parable and allegory have been the subject of
much recent discussion. See pages 60-62 below.

[12] Godet, 379.

For Godet, Jesus is the shepherd.[13] His Jewish-Christian followers, such as the blind man of chapter 9, are the sheep,[14] and the sheepfold represents the theocracy. The thieves and robbers are the Pharisees, who, by hypocrisy and audacity succeeded in climbing into the sheepfold and "in establishing within this spiritual enclosure an authority unsanctioned by any commission from God."[15] Godet adds that "In fact, nothing in the law justified the mission which this party arrogated to itself, and the despotic power it exercised in Israel."[16] The door designates the legitimate entrance, divinely instituted, through which the Messiah—the Shepherd—enters.[17] The gatekeeper is John the Baptist, "for it was he whom God raised up in Israel for the express purpose of announcing the Messiah, and introducing Him into the theocracy."[18]

The allegory extends beyond 10:1–5 to include 10:7–18. For example, the wolf of verse 12, like the thieves and robbers, represents the Pharisees, that is, "the principle which is positively hostile to the Messiah and the kingdom of God,"[19] while the hireling signifies "the legitimate authorities in Israel, the priests and Levites, the appointed teachers of the law, whose position made it their duty to fulfil the task accomplished by the self-sacrifice of Jesus."[20] In his allegorical interpretation, therefore, Godet assumes that the elements of the paroimia correspond directly to characters within the historical tale of the gospel narrative.

Alongside his allegorical interpretation, however, Godet views the passage 10:1–18 as a true-to-life account of pastoral life in the ancient Mediterranean area.[21] He even accounts for the discrepancies between 10:1–5, in which the sheep are led out of the fold, and 10:9, in which they move in and out freely, by attributing the former to an early morning scene and the latter to a scene at midday.[22] Nor does he rule out the biblical background, for he points to the association of the shepherd image with God and the Messiah in Isa 11:11, Ezekiel 34 and Zechariah 11.[23] The allegorical, pastoral, and biblical elements all therefore contribute to his interpretation of the paroimia as a passage depicting Jesus as the Messiah, announced by the Baptist, who has come into the Jewish

---

13 Ibid., 380.
14 Ibid., 382.
15 Ibid., 380.
16 Ibid.
17 Ibid.
18 Ibid., 381.
19 Ibid., 392.
20 Ibid.
21 Ibid., 380.
22 Ibid., 386.
23 Ibid., 379.

theocracy in order to save his Jewish-Christian followers from the control of those evil usurpers of authority, the Pharisees.

A more recent example of allegorical interpretation is to be found in the analysis of John 10 by A. J. Simonis. Whereas Godet's interpretation remained largely within the confines of events narrated within the gospel itself, Simonis attempts a complex, far-ranging allegorical analysis which draws on material from the Hebrew Bible, Josephus, the rest of the New Testament, the Apocrypha, and other literature. His is a strongly historical interpretation, which argues that the *paroimia* draws its terms and structure from the political realities and events of Jesus' day. Hence he sees 10:1–5 as a genuine saying of Jesus, though conveyed by the narrator, who has added the interpretation in verses 7–18.[24]

Simonis argues that the passage is an allusion to a failed attempt by the Zealots (the thieves and robbers)[25] to enter into the temple (the sheepfold)[26] by force ("another way"[27]). This is deplored by Jesus, who asserts that only he (the shepherd)[28] can free the sheep (the Jews, Israel)[29] from the narrow theocracy represented by the temple.[30] Jesus is allowed to enter by the gatekeeper of the temple, who was probably a high priest,[31] and perhaps Caiaphas himself.[32] The rest of the chapter (vv. 7–18) also refers to this same situation.[33]

Although Simonis too situates the pastoral image in the context of everyday life in ancient Palestine,[34] he looks to the usage of this language in biblical and post–biblical Jewish literature for clues to its meaning in the *paroimia*. He relies especially on *1 Enoch* 88–90, in which, he argues, pastoral language is connected with the temple. He also draws on Isa 6:9–10, whose use of the images of sight and blindness, hearing and understanding, is mirrored in the themes of chapters 9 and 10 in the Fourth Gospel and, in Simonis' view, may even be the source of their juxtaposition in this text.[35] Finally, Simonis argues that though the *paroimia* as uttered by Jesus was a clear reference to the specific political situation of his time, it was reinterpreted by the evangelist in order to be meaningful for

---

[24] Simonis, 192–93.
[25] Ibid., 127–42.
[26] Ibid., 120–27.
[27] Ibid., 142–53.
[28] Ibid., 144.
[29] Ibid., 125.
[30] Ibid.
[31] Ibid., 158.
[32] Ibid., 157.
[33] See Simonis, 194–318 for complete analysis.
[34] Ibid., 97.
[35] Ibid., 198.

his readers who may not have been familiar with the Zealot uprising and similar events of the time of Jesus. In this way, the *paroimia* is given a broader application to the relationship between Jesus and his Jewish opponents as a group.[36] Therefore Simonis, in contrast to Godet, sees the elements of the *paroimia* as corresponding initially to historical figures active politically in the time of Jesus, and only secondarily to the characters within the gospel narrative.

A different tack is taken by J. Louis Martyn, who has argued that "the parables [in 10:1–5] and their interpretations [in 10:7–30] must be taken together as an allegory" which would have been understood in the first instance by the members of the Johannine community, by virtue of their common history.[37] Martyn therefore interprets the *paroimia* in the context of the ecclesiological tale, identifying the sheep as the Johannine community; the strangers/thieves/robbers/wolf as the Jewish authorities who kill, destroy, snatch away, and scatter the Johannine community; the hireling as the secretly believing "rulers" who abandon the Johannine community when it is endangered; and the Good Shepherd as "Jesus, as he is active through Johannine evangelists who are prepared to face martyrdom for the community...."[38]

Finally, we may consider the analysis offered by John Painter.[39] Although Painter refers to the *paroimia* as a parable, his interpretation is similar to those of Godet and Simonis in the sense that he explicitly attempts to define the various elements of the passage. In his view, the passage, like the gospel as a whole, must be read on two levels simultaneously: "straightforwardly it is the story of Jesus; and at the reflected level we discern the story of the Johannine community."[40] Painter, therefore, reads the passage within the contexts of both the historical and the ecclesiological tales.

Within the story of Jesus, Painter suggests, the shepherd clearly represents Jesus,[41] while the doorkeeper appears to represent John the Baptist.[42] Within the story of the Johannine community, however, the shepherd may in fact represent the leaders of the community, while the doorkeeper represents Jesus, who admits the church leaders into their positions of leadership within the community. The sheep represent the Johannine community itself.[43] The thieves and robbers in turn represent the Jewish leaders who rejected not only the blind man of the

---

36 Ibid., 170.

37 J. Louis Martyn, *The Gospel of John in Christian History* (New York: Paulist, 1978) 117.

38 Ibid., 116.

39 John Painter, "Tradition, History and Interpretation in John 10," *Shepherd Discourse* (ed. Johannes Beutler and R. T. Fortna; Cambridge: Cambridge University Press, 1991) 53–74.

40 Ibid., 58.

41 Ibid., 57.

42 Ibid., 58.

43 Ibid., 60.

gospel, but also Jesus as well as the Johannine community as a whole.[44] The wolf of John 10:12 stands for the false teachers who have created a schism in the Johannine community.[45] Finally, the hireling refers to Peter, or rather, "a more formal institutional authority, such as Peter represents."[46]

Painter and Martyn read the ecclesiological level as the primary locus of meaning of the *paroimia*. This is in line with their understanding of the intended audience of John 10 (and indeed, one would surmise, the gospel as a whole) as the Johannine community itself, and perhaps "waverers in the synagogue" as well.[47] This reading contrasts with those of Simonis and Godet, who draw heavily on the narrative context of the *paroimia* in order to develop a historical reading of the passage.

Unlike the readings discussed above, those of Hugo Odeberg and Karl Martin Fischer virtually disregard both the immediate narrative context of the *paroimia* and the history of the Johannine church. Odeberg reads the passage in the context of his understanding of Johannine theology and of parallels from rabbinic and gnostic literature, almost all of which postdate the Fourth Gospel. He therefore identifies the sheepfold with "the Divine-Spiritual World into which Jesus seeks to lead men through his coming into the 'world'...The sheep are those who 'listen to his voice....' "[48] The thief is the devil and his kin, and the gatekeeper, the Father.[49] Hence Odeberg's analysis draws parallels between the elements of the *paroimia* and characters and images in the Fourth Gospel. However, he bypasses the historical tale and instead focuses on features of what we have labelled the cosmological tale.

Similar in some ways is the analysis of Karl Martin Fischer, who, like Odeberg, situates the *paroimia* in the context of early Christian gnosticism. For Fischer, the sheepfold is the World of Darkness, the shepherd is the Redeemer, and the sheep are the redeemed. The thief or robber is any potential leader who comes from the World of Darkness.[50] The gatekeeper is more difficult to identify, but may be described as the one appointed by the World of Light, from which the Redeemer came, to guard the door of the World of Darkness. Possible identifications are the Valentinian Horos and/or the Watchers who have been sent by the evil forces to prevent anyone from the World of Light from

---

[44] Ibid., 58.

[45] Ibid., 63.

[46] Ibid., 64.

[47] Ibid., 62.

[48] Hugo Odeberg, *The Fourth Gospel* (Uppsala, 1929; reprinted: Amsterdam: B.R. Grüner, 1968) 313.

[49] Ibid., 328.

[50] Fischer, "Christus," 356–57.

entering.[51] According to Fischer, the elements of the *paroimia* are not to be identified with characters in the Johannine narrative or concepts in Johannine theology per se, but with metaphors and ideas of early gnostic redeemer myths.

Despite differences in interpretation, the allegorical approaches share the methodological assumption that the elements of the *paroimia*, and the interrelationships among them, correspond to some structure outside the *paroimia* itself, either within the historical tale of the gospel, or outside it, in the political or theological background of first-century Judaism and Christianity.

Most recent commentators, however, discount the allegorical approach, preferring to describe the *paroimia* as one, or even more than one, parable. John Quasten, for one, considers the Johannine term *paroimia* to be equivalent to the Synoptic παραβολή, so that the "parabolic character of the figurative discourse is indicated by the word alone."[52]

The move away from considering the *paroimia* to be allegory may be attributed to a great degree to Adolf Jülicher's influential analysis of the parables of Jesus.[53] Jülicher argued that the historical Jesus, a Galilean preacher, would not have spoken in allegories.[54] Rather, he spoke in parables which had only one basic point of comparison and drew many of their details not from the intended message but from their everyday, realistic settings.[55] It should be pointed out, however, that Jülicher considered our *paroimia* to be not a parable, but an allegory, because of what he perceived to be its artificial and contrived nature.[56]

Following Jülicher's definitions of parable and allegory, though not his judgment regarding the passage at hand, those commentators who for various reasons attributed the *paroimia* to Jesus rather than to the evangelist were predisposed against the allegorical interpretation and in favor of considering the *paroimia* to be a pure parable, though perhaps with some "allegorical allusions."[57] Another factor in their opting for the parabolic option may have been the artificiality of some of the attempts at allegorical explanations.[58]

---

[51] Ibid., 258.

[52] Quasten, 9. J. A. T. Robinson ("The Parable of John 10:1–5," *ZNW* 46 [1955] 233–40) has argued that in fact the *paroimia* originally consisted of two parables, the remnants of which are to be found in 1–3a and 3b–5.

[53] Adolf Jülicher, *Die Gleichnisreden Jesu*, vol. 2. (Tübingen, 1910; reprinted: Darmstadt: Wissenschaftliche Buchgesellschaft, 1969).

[54] See C. H. Dodd, *The Parables of the Kingdom* (Glasgow: Fontana, 1961) 16.

[55] Jülicher, *Gleichnisreden*, 1.22, 74.

[56] Ibid., 1.115.

[57] As Quasten, 153, notes, "certain lineaments of the picture...exhibit a greater or lesser parallel to the attitude of Jesus towards the Pharisees. Such allegorical allusions do not exceed the limits of what is customary in the Synoptics. We could here...speak of a 'parabole allégorisante.' "

[58] Ibid., 151–3; Simonis, 96, is aware of these arguments but argues that one should not make an *a priori* assumption on this issue.

The *a priori* assumption that 10:1–5 is a parable affects the way in which scholars approach the passage and the interpretation which they give. First, it suggests that the passage takes its imagery and many of its details, as well as its narrative structure, from the everyday situation which it describes. Second, it requires scholars to look for only one or two main points of comparison, rather than a point-by-point correspondence between the elements of the *paroimia* and its interpretation. As a result, many of the details which appear to be extraneous to the main point of the parable are thought to have been included only for the purposes of ornamentation.

The interpretation of John Quasten provides a good illustration of this approach.[59] Before Quasten begins to consider the meaning and trend of thought of the passage, he discusses its "Palestinian background:"

> The sheep, which during the day are out on the pasture, are driven in the evening to an enclosure surrounded by a low stone wall or hedge of thorns, to protect them against wild beasts, robbers, and thieves. Several flocks are enclosed in a fold of this type. The watch over them is entrusted to one or more shepherds, according to the number of the sheep. This watchman is the θυρωρός of the parable. The other shepherds, relieved of further duty, seek repose in their dwellings. In the morning they return. Each one summons his flock with a distinctive call. The sheep know this call and follow their shepherd outside. There he counts his sheep and puts himself at their head, leading them to pasture.[60]

His conclusion is that "our parable is true to nature in every particular."[61] He refutes Jülicher's suggestion that the parable describes "unnatural conditions" by accusing Jülicher of being ignorant of Palestinian customs.[62]

It is extremely difficult to argue conclusively either that the *paroimia* does, or does not, provide an accurate description of pastoral practices in ancient Palestine. It will be noted, however, that Quasten's description of these practices is not independent but is derived almost entirely from the structure and elements of the *paroimia* itself. As supporting evidence he cites Strack-Billerbeck[63] and various specific studies which themselves are not independent of the gospel but

---

[59] Quasten, 151–52.
[60] Ibid., 6.
[61] Ibid.
[62] Ibid.
[63] See Ibid.; he cites Str-B 2.537.

rather assume the literal accuracy of the *paroimia*.[64] As further support, he notes that D. Buzy saw a sheepfold of the kind which Quasten describes while travelling in Palestine.[65]

Though the nature of pastoral practices in ancient Palestine cannot be determined with any accuracy, it is clear that Quasten assumes that they are reflected in this passage. Quasten and other exegetes make an *a priori* assumption that this *paroimia* and indeed the entire discourse convey the genuine words of the historical Jesus.[66] Since the historical Jesus could only have spoken in parables, this passage must be a parable. Since parables were rooted in everyday experience, and since Jesus always spoke truthfully, this passage must surely be an accurate reflection of shepherding practices in ancient Palestine. This conclusion completes the exegetical circle.

According to this explanation, as in the allegorical interpretation, the elements and structure of the *paroimia* do correspond to some structure outside the passage itself, in this case the structure of everyday pastoral life in ancient Palestine. At the same time, however, the meaning of the passage, as opposed to the source of its language and imagery, is found in the gospel itself.

The assumption that the *paroimia* is a parable rather than an allegory obviates the need for specific identification of each element as well as of the overall structure, since these are seen to stem from the pastoral context of the parable. Instead, one or at the most two central points are sought. For Quasten, the *paroimia* has two essential characteristics: the entrance by the door and the confidential relation between shepherd and flock. "Both of these points serve to set up a contrast between shepherd and non-shepherd, the thief or robber. In this contrast the real basic significance of the parable must be sought."[67] Therefore the term of comparison is the behavior of the sheep: they follow the shepherd; they do not follow the thief.

The referent of this comparison is to be sought in the context of the passage as a whole, and particularly chapter 9. The shepherd is clearly Jesus, the sheep are those who follow him, like the blind man of chapter 9. The thieves and robbers are therefore the Pharisees, who stand against both Jesus and the blind

[64] Cf., for example, A. M. Rihbany, *The Syrian Christ* (2d. ed.; London: Andrew Melrose, 1920) 212, and W. M. Thomson, *The Land and the Book* (London: Nelson and Sons: 1891) 202–5.

[65] Quasten, 7; he cites D. Buzy, *Introduction aux Paraboles Evangeliques* (Paris, 1912) 450ff.

[66] Quasten, 165–69. For a consideration of the question of whether the *paroimia* originated with Jesus or was constructed by the evangelist, see Painter, "Tradition," 56–58.

[67] Quasten, 153.

man in that chapter.[68] All of the other details are not germane to the meaning but are added only for verisimilitude.[69]

Thus the main purpose of the parable is to brand the Pharisees, "who regard themselves as the real leaders of the people," as "false leaders and as guides to error."[70] Quasten formulates the comparison in this way:

> Just as the sheep, with an unfailing instinct, recognize and follow their shepherd but do not follow a robber and an interloper, so it is quite in accord with nature that the man born blind and others of this kind do not obey the false leaders of the people, in whom, with the sure vision of the unspoilt popular mind, they recognize their corrupters, whilst in Jesus they see their rightful shepherd and join him.[71]

Quasten's views are shared by many commentators. One exception is Bultmann, who, though he agrees that the *paroimia* is a parable, offers an interpretation which is similar to the allegorical reading of Fischer. For Bultmann, the shepherd is the evangelist's version of the Gnostic Revealer, who has come into the world (the fold) to save those who will obey him.[72] He is contrasted with the thief/robber, who is not to be identified with a specific entity but rather stands for "anyone who unlawfully claims to have control over the flock, i.e.,...every corrupter of the faithful." Hence, he argues, Odeberg's suggestion that the thief is the devil is wrong.[73] Bultmann, like Quasten, believes that it is inappropriate to identify the gatekeeper or the door, who are mentioned merely to give greater vividness to the scene.[74]

The parabolic interpretation of the *paroimia* is problematic for two reasons. The first concerns the attempt to situate the language and images of the passage in the everyday experiences of rural life in ancient Palestine. No doubt the intended readers of this gospel were familiar with sheep, shepherds, and sheepfolds, as well as with the routines and hazards of pastoral life. Nevertheless, this does not in itself demonstrate that the structure of the *paroimia* and the specific language used to express the relationships among its principal elements derive from the pastoral situation itself. Indeed, this language is thoroughly Johannine, paralleled throughout the Fourth Gospel. For example, though

---

[68] Ibid.
[69] Ibid., 151.
[70] Ibid., 153.
[71] Ibid.
[72] Bultmann, 373.
[73] Ibid., 371, n.3.
[74] Ibid., 372, n.2.

Brown may note, following Bernard,[75] that "Palestinian shepherds frequently have pet names for their favorite sheep, 'Long-ears,' 'White-nose,' etc.,"[76] the "name" is an important Johannine theological concept.[77] Not only the sheep within chapter 10 but also the disciples (e.g., 1:42) and Mary Magdalene (20:16) are called by name. The acts of hearing and heeding Jesus' voice, and of following him, are not limited to the sheep in 10:1–5 but are also characteristic of those who believe in Jesus throughout the gospel (cf. 5:24–25; 1:37, 38, 43; 8:12; 12:26; 21:19, 22).[78]

These parallels have not been lost on commentators, who utilize them in the course of their interpretations. While the parallels do not rule out the possibility that the structure of the *paroimia* takes its cue from Palestinian pastoral practices, they do suggest that the description of these practices has been couched in the language of Johannine theology. This observation serves to qualify Quasten's confident assertion that "Nobody can deny that the picture in vv.1–5 is delineated in harmony with actual life and that it is adequate in itself."[79]

Second, it seems obvious that for many, the judgment regarding genre is an *a priori* one, based, first of all, on a predisposition to see Jesus as the speaker of these words and, second, on assumptions regarding the manner in which a Galilean carpenter might have spoken. There has been, however, some questioning of Jülicher's position concerning the authentic form of Jesus' preaching. Although Jülicher still has his strong supporters,[80] many recent scholars argue that it is necessary to challenge the rigid distinctions Jülicher drew between parable and allegory in Jesus' preaching.[81] Dan O. Via, for example, argues that parable and allegory share many features. Contrary to Jülicher's view,

---

[75] J. H. Bernard, A Critical and Exegetical Commentary on the Gospel According to St. John (Edinburgh: T. and T. Clark, 1928) 2.350.

[76] AB 1.385.

[77] Cf. for example 20:31.

[78] The application of authentic life-setting as a criterion for distinguishing parable from allegory breaks down, as noted by G. B. Caird, since some parables "rely for their effect on a startling departure from normal procedure." Examples are to be found in Matt 18:24, 20:9, and Luke 14:18. See G. B. Caird, the Language and Imagery of the Bible (London: Duckworth, 1980) 164.

[79] Quasten, 152.

[80] For example, Joachim Jeremias, The Parables of Jesus (rev. ed.; London: SCM, 1972); Eta Linnemann, Parables of Jesus: Introduction and Exposition (London: SPCK, 1966) 8.

[81] AB 1.390. Cf. also his article "Parable and Allegory Reconsidered," NovT 5 (1962) 36–45; Dan Otto Via Jr. The Parables: Their Literary and Existential Dimension (Philadelphia: Fortress, 1967) 2; Mary Ann Tolbert Perspectives on the Parables: An Approach to Multiple Interpretations (Philadelphia: Fortress, 1979) 28; J. Arthur Baird, The Justice of God in the Teaching of Jesus (Philadelphia: Westminster, 1963) 26–28; Hans-Josef Klauck, Allegorie und Allegorese in synoptischen Gleichnistexten (NTAbh 13; Münster: Aschendorff, 1978).

Via states, parables cannot be restricted to a single point of comparison.[82] Like allegories, parables may contain symbolic images brought from another world of thought. What distinguishes a parable is that it exhibits an internal cohesion that is not characteristic of allegories.[83] Other scholars, however, see no opposition between allegory and parable. Bernard Brendan Scott, for example, suggests that parables as a genre can be allegorical, metaphorical, or mixed.[84] G. B. Caird argues that parable and allegory, far from representing distinct genres, are in fact partial synonyms.[85]

The breakdown of Jülicher's distinctions has led some scholars to attempt an analysis of the passage that is independent of the definition of *paroimia* as either parable or allegory. Rudolf Schnackenburg,[86] following his student Odo Kiefer, argues that in fact the passage is neither a parable nor an allegory, but rather a puzzle or a riddle, constituting a genre all its own.[87] On the basis of a detailed literary analysis, Kiefer concludes that 10:1–18 as a whole is in the discourse style of the evangelist, who has situated the discourse in the historical situation of the life of Jesus, and that it belongs to a literary genre characteristic of this evangelist, namely the *Bildrede,* in which the image or picture is completely subordinate to the point to which it refers.

Another suggestion has been made by Robert Kysar. Kysar had referred to the *paroimia* as an allegory in his work entitled *John's Story of Jesus,* on the grounds that it is different from the story parables that we know from the other gospels. In contrast to the Synoptics, John's method was to employ longer and more complex metaphors, for which the term allegory is the most descriptive.[88] In a more recent study of John 10, however, Kysar has explored the Johannine use of metaphor in this chapter in greater detail and, significantly, has declined to label the *paroimia* as either allegory or parable, although he does note the similarities between these Johannine metaphors and the Synoptic parables.[89]

---

[82] Via, *The Parables,* 17.

[83] Ibid., 25.

[84] Bernard Brandon Scott, *Hear Then the Parable: A Commentary on the Parables of Jesus* (Minneapolis: Fortress, 1989) 44.

[85] Caird, *Language,* 167. Caird argues that the distinction must be drawn not between parable and allegory, but between allegory and allegorization, which he defines as the imposition on a story of "hidden meanings which the original author neither intended nor envisaged" (*Language,* 165). This distinction too has its drawbacks, however, not the least of which is the difficulty, if not the impossibility of determining the intention of the original author or speaker of the parables.

[86] Schnack. 2.284–85.

[87] Kiefer, *Die Hirtenrede,* 14–15.

[88] Kysar, *Story,* 51.

[89] Robert Kysar, "Johannine Metaphor—Meaning and Function: A Literary Case Study of John 10:1–18," *Semeia* 53 (1991) 81–111.

Even if one could determine with certainty whether Jesus spoke in allegories as well as in parables, this would not necessarily determine the genre of the *paroimia* in John 10:1–5, since it is certainly possible that these words did not originate with the historical Jesus but rather with the evangelist. Nor would it mean that the implied reader would have drawn on these categories as an aid in interpreting the passage. Whereas modern scholars see the labelling of the passage as a *paroimia* as a signal to compare the passage with examples of figurative modes of speech from outside the gospel, it may be that the implied reader would look for comparison within the Fourth Gospel itself. This possibility and its methodological implications will be explored in our own analysis in the following chapter.

CONTEXT OF 10:1–5

John 10:7–18. In addition to identifying the preceding five verses as a *paroimia*, the narrator's comment in 10:6 implies that the reader should look in the first place to the context of the passage for help in its explication. The scholarly discussion of the context of the *paroimia* focuses on two main questions. The first concerns the relationship between 10:1–6 and 10:7–18,[90] and the second, the relationship between chapters 9 and 10.

The structure of chapter 10 implies a connection between the *paroimia* in 10:1–5 and Jesus' discourse in the remainder of the chapter, which utilizes some of the pastoral imagery of 10:1–5. There are, however, obstacles to understanding 10:7–18 as a straightforward explanation of the *paroimia*. In the first place, 10:7–18 confuses matters by identifying Jesus as both the shepherd (10:11) and the gate or door (10:7, 9). As an aspect of Johannine christology, this dual identification is not troubling, since these are only two of many images used for Jesus in this gospel. But for the purposes of interpreting 10:1–5, it is awkward to have Jesus as both shepherd and door. A second obstacle concerns the introduction of new characters into the pastoral setting. The "thief and bandit" of 10:1 is displaced in 10:13 from the role of antagonist by the hireling and the wolf, whose activities threaten the herd out at pasture (10:12–13). Despite these difficulties, however, most scholars acknowledge some continuity between 10:1–5 and 10:7–18.

---

[90] Many see 10:18 as the end of the pericope, but some see it as extending to verse 21. See for example, C. K. Barrett, *The Gospel According to St. John* (2d ed.; Philadelphia: Westminster, 1978) 367; Quasten. Others prefer to deal with the chapter as a whole, e.g., J. E. Bruns, "The Discourse on the Good Shepherd and the Rite of Ordination," *AER* 149 (1963) 386–91.

Rudolf Bultmann deals with the difficulties presented by 10:1–18 in his characteristic manner, which is by appealing to dislocation theory. His reconstruction of chapter 10 presents the following order: 10:22–26, 11–13, 1–10, 14–18, and 27–30.[91] He argues that the *paroimia* was followed in the evangelist's revelatory discourse source by an interpretation which took up its images as metaphors.[92] Some of this has been preserved in verses 7–10, 14–18 and 27–30, with the addition of a few glosses from the evangelist's own hand. Among these he includes the troublesome "door" references in 10:7, 9.[93] Hence, some of the content of 10:7–18 may legitimately be used in interpreting the *paroimia*, and this is what Bultmann does.[94]

Bultmann's rearrangement of this passage has not found overwhelming favor with other Johannine scholars.[95] Brown criticizes Bultmann quite sharply for violating the deliberate plan which informs John 10 as a whole.[96] Brown sees vv. 7ff. as a series of three allegorical explanations of 10:1–5,[97] some of which may represent later expansions of Jesus' own remarks. These explanations are centered on the door or gate (vv. 7–10), the shepherd (vv. 11–18), and the sheep (vv. 26–30), all of which are important terms in the *paroimia*.[98] As a series of explanations, carefully arranged by the evangelist, they are therefore important keys to the meaning of the *paroimia* in its present context.

John Quasten expresses a similar view. He regards 10:7–10 and 10:11–18 as genuine discourses uttered by Jesus. Each of these represents a different interpretation of the *paroimia*.[99] They are not, however, rigorous, methodical interpretations.[100] Though they explain the *paroimia* and link up with its main elements,[101] they do not remain within the bounds of the *paroimia* but develop its themes independently. They therefore shed light on the *paroimia* from two different perspectives.[102] Quasten's understanding of the relationship between

---

[91] Bultmann, 375.

[92] For detailed discussion, see Dwight Moody Smith, Jr. *The Composition and Order of the Fourth Gospel* (New Haven: Yale University Press, 1965) 15–34.

[93] Bultmann, 375.

[94] In his own interpretation of the *paroimia*, he does rely to some extent on his own, somewhat idiosyncratic understanding of 7–10, 14–18, and 27–30, suggesting that there is some continuity of meaning. Cf. Bultmann, 373.

[95] Dislocation theory is adopted, however, by John D. Turner, "The History of Religions Background of John 10," *Shepherd Discourse*, 34.

[96] AB 1.390.

[97] In this he follows Robinson, who sees the *paroimia* as composed of two separate parables of Jesus. See Robinson, "Parable," 233–40.

[98] AB 1.391.

[99] Quasten, 167.

[100] Ibid., 154.

[101] Ibid., 156.

[102] Ibid.

the *paroimia* and vv. 7–18 is shared by numerous other scholars.[103] Hence in most discussions it is assumed that vv. 7–18 may be used selectively in interpreting vv. 1–5.

John 9. The second contextual issue concerns the location of the *paroimia* and indeed chapter 10 as a whole after chapter 9. This is an issue because of the abrupt change of topic and imagery between these two chapters. Whereas chapter 9 revolves around the contrast between light and darkness, sight and blindness, chapter 10 contrasts the shepherd and the thief. Furthermore, despite the links implied by their juxtaposition, there is no explicit connection made between these chapters until 10:21, which mentions the healing of the blind man.

These problems caused some older exegetes, such as Wellhausen, to argue that there is no connection at all between chapter 9 and 10, and that the latter therefore stands completely isolated from any context or background.[104] Others, such as Hugo Odeberg, simply disregard chapter 9 in their analyses.[105] As might be expected, Bultmann deals with the problem of context by relocating chapter 10, in its revised order as discussed above, to the end of a complex of passages drawn from chapters 9, 8, and 12.[106] In this way, chapters 9 and 10 are not completely distanced, but it is no longer necessary to try to find a direct relationship between them. Neither of these approaches is accepted by the majority of recent scholars. Even Rudolf Schnackenburg, who is moderately enthusiastic about the idea of transposing chapter 10 from its present context, sees strong ties between chapters 9 and 10, so strong that he would relocate 10:1–18 between 9:29 and 9:30.[107]

Most scholars find both narrative and thematic connections between these two chapters. All agree on the continuity of setting and audience between chapters 9 and 10.[108] Theological continuity is suggested by C. H. Dodd, who sees the theme of judgment in each of the chapters.[109] Many exegetes find more specific thematic connections, arguing that in fact the figures of "sheep,"

103 Kiefer, *Hirtenrede*, 15; Simonis, 330–31; Barrett, *Gospel*, 370.

104 Julius Wellhausen, *Das Evangelium Johannis* (Berlin: Georg Reimer, 1908) 47.

105 Odeberg, *Gospel*, 313.

106 9:1–41; 8:12; 12:44–50; 8:21–29; 12:34–36. See Bultmann, ix.

107 Schnack. 2.177.

108 See Aileen Guilding, *The Fourth Gospel and Jewish Worship* (Oxford: Clarendon, 1960) 127–39; See also Quasten, 4–5. The consensus on this point is considered by the editors of *Shepherd Discourse* to be one of the most important results of the two-year study of this chapter. See "Introduction," *Shepherd Discourse*, 3. See also Jan A. Du Rand, "A syntactical and narratological reading of John 10 in coherence with chapter 9," *Shepherd Discourse*, 94–115.

109 Dodd, 358.

"shepherd," and "thief" in 10:1–5 correspond directly to the major characters of chapter 9. The shepherd is Jesus, the sheep are exemplified by the man born blind who has heard Jesus' voice and followed him,[110] and the thief, bandit, stranger, of 10:1, 5 is a collective metaphor for the Pharisees and other Jewish leaders who in chapter 9 stand in opposition to Jesus and to those who believe in him.[111]

This brief summary indicates that despite the obstacles, there is general agreement among scholars that it is necessary to take the entire context of the *paroimia*—including the verses which follow it, the chapter which precedes it, and indeed the gospel as a whole—into account in any discussion. This conclusion is not very striking, since it seems self-evident that all readers—whether scholars or not—should, and indeed do, take the immediate context into account when trying to understand a particular story or passage.[112] What is interesting to note is that, by and large, the scholarly readers surveyed have all highlighted the same features of the *paroimia's* context, namely the relationships among the major characters, which are seen as parallel to the connections among the characters within the *paroimia*.

SUMMARY

Context and Genre of the Paroimia. Our survey has pointed to some general similarities among the various readings of this passage. Virtually all scholars make selective use of 10:7–18. This process of selection is clearest with respect to the dual identification of Jesus as both gate (10:7, 9) and shepherd (10:11). Some scholars have identified Jesus as the gate in the *paroimia*, arguing that the shepherd is a collective image for the disciples who enter the fold by means of Jesus.[113] Most scholars reject this, however, arguing that despite the "door words" in 10:7, 9, the image which dominates the chapter is that of Jesus as shepherd, and that Jesus is therefore the intended referent of "shepherd" in 10:1–5.[114]

Second, almost all scholars make explicit or implicit assumptions regarding genre, though the views of Schnackenburg, Kysar, and others suggest that this trend may now be changing. With some exceptions, most recent exegetes classify

---

[110] Quasten, 153.

[111] Ibid.; Martin, "John 10:1–10," 171; Dodd, 359; Augustin George, "Je suis la porte des brebis," BVC 51 (1963) 21.

[112] For a discussion of the importance of sequence on the reading process, see Wolfgang Iser, "The Reading Process: A Phenomenological Approach," *Reader-Response Criticism,* 52–57.

[113] J. E. Bruns, "The Discourse on the Good Shepherd and the Rite of Ordination," AER 149 (1963) 386–91.

[114] Schnack. 2.289.

the passage as a parable. It is worth noting that while the decision regarding genre may affect how the scholars approach the task of interpreting the *paroimia*, it does not for the most part affect their results significantly.

Third, the majority of scholars, whether they see the *paroimia* as a parable or as an allegory, in fact do attempt to identify the four major elements of the passage. The areas of disagreement concern whether or not to assign a meaning to the door and/or the gatekeeper, which some like Quasten would suggest are present only for ornamental reasons. But we have already indicated above that in fact the door and the doorkeeper are not independent elements; rather their interpretation is dependent on, or derives from, one's understanding of the "sheepfold." Therefore the attempt to, or the decision not to, identify these elements is not really crucial in determining the meaning of the *paroimia*, at least for the scholars whose views we have surveyed.

Finally, all agree that the implied author is drawing on, and presumably assuming on the part of his audience, information and knowledge of events, concepts, and literature from outside the gospel itself. Most scholars make at least passing reference to biblical background. Some draw extensively on apocryphal (Simonis), gnostic (Bultmann, Fischer, Odeberg), targumic,[115] and/or rabbinic (Odeberg, Derrett) materials as well.[116] Though some of these bodies of literature postdate the Fourth Gospel, the assumption is made that the images and trends of thought they express pre-date the collections of literature in which they are found.

Readings and Meanings of John 10:1–5. With regard to the precise meaning assigned to the *paroimia* and its constituent elements, we may discern three trends of thought. The dominant trend contends that whether the passage is allegory or parable, both, or neither, it is its placement after chapter 9 which is most important for determining its meaning. Thus, the contrast between the shepherd and the thief in the *paroimia* must be seen as parallel to that between Jesus and the Pharisees in chapter 9, which mirrors that in the gospel narrative as a whole. This consideration plays a part even in the allegorical and highly speculative reconstruction of the background of the *paroimia* undertaken by Simonis.[117] Furthermore, in this approach a parallel is drawn between the intimate relationship between the shepherd and the sheep in the *paroimia* and

---

115 Fréderic Manns, *L'Evangile de Jean à la lumière du Judaïsme*, (Studium Biblicum Franciscanum, Analecta 33; Jerusalem: Franciscan Printing Press, 1991) 227–33.

116 There has also recently been a suggestion that John 10 betrays John's knowledge of the Synoptic Gospels. See M. Sabbe, "John 10 and its Relationship to the Synoptic Gospels," *Shepherd Discourse*, 75–93.

117 Simonis, 189–90.

that between Jesus and the man born blind, a believer, in chapter 9. By default, the sheepfold, the locus of activity of the shepherd, thief, and sheep, must be the temple, the Jewish community, or the Jewish theocracy.

These parallels are present not only in chapter 9 but within the gospel narrative as a whole. The relationship between the shepherd and the sheep mirrors that between Jesus and the disciples, in which Jesus leads and the disciples follow; the disciples hear Jesus' voice and heed him. Similarly, the hostility between Jesus and the Pharisees is similar to the contrast between the shepherd and the thief, since that hostility concerns to some degree jurisdiction or authority over the sheep or the believers. Finally, the persecution which the disciples suffer, or will suffer, at the hands of the Jewish leadership may be likened to the death and destruction which the thief/robber aims to inflict on the sheep.

In other words, scholars following this line of interpretation situate the passage squarely in the context of the relationships and sequence of events which comprise the historical tale of the gospel. They see the relationships among the three major characters of the *paroimia* as parallel to the relationships among the three major characters or groups of characters in the Fourth Gospel, namely Jesus, the Pharisees, and the disciples, and the conflict in 10:1-5 as concerning the central issue of the historical tale, namely belief and unbelief.

A second trend is to interpret the *paroimia* ecclesiologically, that is, within the structure and concerns of the ecclesiological tale. That these two trends are not mutually exclusive is illustrated by E. C. Hoskyns, who argues that the passage must be read on both levels:

In the immediate literary context the Pharisees are, as had been noted above, the blasphemous opponents of Jesus, and the reader is intended to recognize them again in the thieves and robbers of the parable. This is, of course, quite essential to the author of the Gospel, for the opposition of the Jews to Jesus was a supreme blasphemy. But blasphemy is not for him exhausted in a single historical occurrence. In the perspective of the Fourth Gospel it is repeated in the opposition of the Jews to the Church, and, what is perhaps more important to him, in the appearance within the Church of those anti-Christs who deny the authority of the historical Jesus, who is *come in the flesh*...But more is involved even than this, for there is no point in human history which lies beyond the horizon of the thieves and robbers of the parable.[118]

---

[118] E. C. Hoskyns and F. N. Davey, *The Fourth Gospel* (London: Faber and Faber, 1947) 368.

Hoskyns therefore expands the horizons of the *paroimia* not only to the original Johannine community but to the Christian experience throughout the ages.

James Martin outlines a different ecclesiological interpretation. He suggests that the passage must be read in the context of the situation of Judaism and Christianity in the period after the destruction of the temple in 70 C.E. In this period, he suggests, the Jews' loss of nationhood led the rabbis at Jamnia to redefine the community along rigid lines, that is, as a closed community. In contrast, Jesus functioned as an open door, around whom a community open to both Jews and Gentiles was created. The conflict depicted in the *paroimia* therefore represents the conflict between these open and closed communities in the post-70 period.[119] Like Hoskyns, however, Martin suggests that "although Johannine metaphors arise out of a specific and complex historical situation, they are stated in such a form as to transcend their original historical situation and to function in other sociologically similar situations."[120]

CONCLUSION

Even the most intrepid reader-response critic must exhibit some humility with respect to his or her ability to determine, or second-guess, accurately the response of the implied reader to a text from which he or she is so far removed in time, in space, and in world view. Yet it may be suggested that the implied readers' response to, or interpretation of, this *paroimia* is by no means exhausted by its parallels to the historical and ecclesiological tales of the gospel narrative. This suggestion is based on two considerations, one general, and one specific.

The general reason has to do with the purpose of the gospel. In light of the role of the cosmological tale as meta-tale, as the broadest frame of reference of both the historical and ecclesiological tales, it may be said that the purpose of the gospel is to lead its readers to view the cosmological tale, which is the locus and context of Johannine soteriology and christology, in and through the narrative. Furthermore, we have seen that many of the most important metaphors for Jesus as savior, such as light, and life, are rooted in the cosmological tale. If the specific episodes and scenes, as well as important christological metaphors, have the cosmological tale as their frame of reference,

---

[119] Martin, "John 10:1–10," 172–73.

[120] Martin (Ibid. 174) says that, therefore, the metaphor does not justify anti-Judaism in order to validate its functioning for Christian faith, although to this reader his interpretation does have an anti-Jewish ring to it.

this should be true also of other, more oblique metaphors with which the Johannine Jesus peppers his discourses.

The specific reason for questioning the adequacy of the historical and ecclesiological interpretations of the *paroimia* lies in the fact that most of the scholarly views we have surveyed, in emphasizing the relationships among shepherd, thief, and sheep, and their parallels to the Johannine Jesus, Jews, and believers on the one hand, and Christian leaders, Jewish leaders, and the Johannine community on the other hand, have paid insufficient attention to the fourth major element of the *paroimia*, namely the sheepfold.

The difficulty in identifying this element of the *paroimia* is indicated by the fact that neither Painter nor Martyn, who identify the other elements in the *paroimia* in the context of the ecclesiological tale, suggests a specific referent for the sheepfold. For scholars whose reading focuses on the meaning of the passage within the historical tale, the specific understanding of the sheepfold derives from their identification of the three main characters of the *paroimia*, and it is therefore seen variously as the temple, Jewish community, or the Jewish theocracy in the historical tale.[121] If this is the case, however, in what sense can it be said that the Pharisees have entered through stealth? Godet addresses this question by saying that the Pharisees have usurped the authority of the priestly class.[122] Because there is no reference to this idea in the gospel, this interpretation is not convincing.

Are the readers led to see Jesus' divinely given task as entering into, and leading the disciples out of, the Jewish community? While it is true that according to 9:22 following Jesus resulted in expulsion from the synagogue,[123] other passages such as 11:1–44 make it clear that such was not the case for all, since Mary and Martha, public followers of Jesus, are comforted by many Jews in their mourning of Lazarus.[124] More important, this limited definition of Jesus' mission does not correspond with other more explicit statements concerning Jesus' mission, which, as we have seen, is generally described in the universal terms of the cosmological tale and not narrowly in terms of leading followers out of Judaism, the temple, or other related entities.

These considerations have been addressed, at least indirectly, by the minority trend which we have uncovered in our survey of the scholarly literature. This trend is represented by Fischer and Odeberg, and, to a lesser extent, by Bultmann. Unlike Quasten and others, they all to varying degrees provide a cosmological reading of the text. For Bultmann and Fischer, the fold is

---

[121] Simonis, 129.

[122] Godet, 380.

[123] See Introduction, p. 4 , note 15.

[124] See Reinhartz, "Narrative to History," 178.

this world into which the Revealer or Redeemer, the shepherd, comes and out of which he leads his followers, the sheep. The thief and robber are those forces which aim to prevent this process from taking place. Odeberg's interpretation differs slightly. For him the fold is the Divine-Spiritual world into which the shepherd, who is also the door, wishes to lead his followers. While such a reading takes seriously the cosmological level of the Fourth Gospel and gives pride of place to the sheepfold, its dissociation of the *paroimia* from its narrative context is evidence of its failure to pick up on the clues provided by the implied author in 10:6.[125]

In conclusion, John 10:6 points its readers to both the genre and the context of 10:1–5 in their attempt to understand the *paroimia* which eluded Jesus' audience within the gospel narrative. This verse has led most scholars to use the historical and/or ecclesiological tale as the frame of reference or interpretive key. Yet it is these two considerations themselves which are the basis for questioning not so much the accuracy of such an interpretation but rather its adequacy. While the historical and ecclesiological interpretations of the *paroimia* do make sense of certain features of the passage, they do not tell the whole, or final, story. Rather, John 10:1–5, as well as its historical and ecclesiological interpretations, can and indeed must, like the rest of the gospel narrative, be situated in the context of the cosmological tale. It is to this task that we now turn.

---

[125] This may be an example of what Meir Sternberg (*The Poetics of Biblical Narrative* [Bloomington: Indiana University Press, 1987] 188) refers to as "illegitimate gap-filling," that is, "one launched and sustained by the reader's subjective concerns (or dictated by more general preconceptions) rather than by the text's own norms and directives." In this case, one suspects that the readings suggested by Odeberg, Fischer, and Bultmann derive more from their general theories concerning gnostic influences on the Fourth Gospel than from specific clues in the narrative itself.

4

JOHN 10:1–5
AND THE COSMOLOGICAL TALE

In this chapter, we, like the commentators surveyed in the previous chapter, shall take our methodological cues from 10:6 and shall first consider the issue of genre, and second, provide an alternative reading based on the structure of relationships within the *paroimia* as well as on its immediate and extended context in the Fourth Gospel.

GENRE REVISITED

In our discussion of the range of scholarly readings of the passage, we noted that most cope with the label *paroimia* which the narrator provides for 10:1–5 by identifying it with one of two types of figurative discourses associated with early Christianity, namely the parable or the allegory. The assumption that the passage belongs to one of these two genres, often made in an *a priori* way, has obvious methodological implications. If the passage is an allegory, then it is the task of the interpreter to find a correspondence between all the elements of the passage on the one hand, and some narrative or theological structure outside the passage—or even outside the gospel—on the other hand. If the passage is a parable, then the interpreter must make a judgment as to which elements contribute to its meaning and which are incidental or ornamental. The former are then interpreted in the context of some structure external to the passage itself.

This strategy works to the extent that it takes seriously the figurative element implied by the term *paroimia*, which invites comparison between the *paroimia* and some plain meaning outside it. However, while the controversy over genre has its primary context in the modern study of the canonical gospels, in particular that field's concern with the form of Jesus' discourses, it would not necessarily have been an issue for the implied reader of the gospel. Rather, one may suggest that the implied reader may have looked to the gospel itself for clues as to how to understand a *paroimia*.

Although the term *paroimia* is applied explicitly only to 10:1–5, the gospel is replete with figurative discourse, symbol, and metaphor. In fact, the disciples' grateful comment in 16:29, "Yes, now you are speaking plainly, not in any figure of speech!" suggests that they, and the implied readers with them, have been engaged in many struggles to decipher the plain meaning of Jesus' words. A first-time reader, reading through the gospel narrative in sequence, might think of Jesus' discussion with Nicodemus, in which the subject is rebirth, or of his encounter with the Samaritan woman, in which he offers her "living water," or of the feeding of the multitudes, after which Jesus, to the chagrin of his Jewish audience, declares himself to be the bread which came down from heaven (6:41). A reader who is reading this gospel for the second or subsequent time would perhaps think of the figure of the vine and the vinedresser in 15:1–8, according to which Jesus is the vine, God the vinedresser (15:1), and the disciples the branches (15:5).

What these examples have in common is that, though tied to the historical framework of the historical tale, they lead the reader to the level of the cosmological tale and offer the latter as the key to understanding the true significance—or plain meaning—of a particular figurative exchange. The figure of the vine and vinedresser in chapter 15 appears in the context of the conflict between Jesus and the ruler of this world (14:30–31). Jesus' words to Nicodemus emphasize the Son of Man's descent from heaven to which he will ascend again (3:13). The Samaritan women and all the Samaritans recognize Jesus as the Savior of the world (4:42). Using these exchanges as a model, it may be suggested that the implied readers will have been led to place other examples of figurative discourse (as well as narrative) not only in the context of the historical tale but in that of the cosmological tale as well.

Such a decision would have been reinforced by allusions to the cosmological tale in 10:7–18. These verses speak explicitly of the abundant, eternal life which the shepherd provides for his sheep (10:10), of the mutual knowledge of Father and Son (10:15), of the Son's power to lay down his life and take it up again (10:17). Discussion of these themes is continued in 10:22–30, in which Jesus accuses the Jews of not belonging to his sheep. They are not among those who "hear my voice." Of the latter, Jesus says, "I know them, and they follow me. I give them eternal life, and they will never perish. No one will snatch them out of my hand" (10:27–28). These verses, which are part of the conclusion to the shepherd/sheep discourse, clearly use the pastoral imagery introduced in 10:1–5 to express Jesus' mission as formulated within the cosmological tale. Though 10:7–30 may not keep strictly to the terms of the *paroimia*, it may be that its direct allusions to the cosmological tale are to be seen as clues to the meaning of the *paroimia* to which it is tied by the structure and pastoral language of the chapter as a whole.

John 9 also leads the reader in this direction, for it places the healing of the blind man, a "historical" event, in the context of the cosmological tale, by seeing it as a manifestation of Jesus' works as "the light of the world" (9:5) who came into this world for judgment (9:39). These comments suggest that the implied readers would have been expected by the gospel, and encouraged by the immediate context of 10:1-5, to look beyond the parallels between the *paroimia* and the historical tale to the parallels between 10:1-5 and the cosmological tale.

If the gospel itself provides the implied reader with the interpretive framework of the *paroimia*, it also leads the reader to a specific strategy for beginning the interpretive task. This strategy is hinted at in 10:7, 9, and 11, in which the Johannine Jesus declares "I am the gate" (10:7, 9) and "I am the good shepherd" (10:11). Though this dual identification is confusing, as we have already noted, it does direct the reader to assign at least one of the central elements of the *paroimia*—the shepherd—to a character outside it, that is, Jesus. This suggests that we are to strive to identify the other elements with characters outside the *paroimia* but within the gospel as well. Such identification can be done on the basis not only of what is said about them in the *paroimia*, aided by 10:7-18, but also by the relationships among them as portrayed in the *paroimia* itself.

Our investigation will therefore begin by looking at each of the elements and the structure of the relationships among them, in the context of the cosmological tale. We will use 10:7ff. as well as the rest of the gospel for help in this task. We will then look at the cosmological interpretation of the *paroimia* as a whole and consider its place in its immediate context between chapters 9 and 11, as well as in the context of the gospel as a whole.

THE ELEMENTS OF THE PAROIMIA

The Shepherd. Within the *paroimia*, the shepherd is defined in relationship to the thief/bandit, to the sheepfold, its door and doorkeeper, and to the sheep. He is contrasted with the thief/bandit/stranger, with respect to his mode of entry into the sheepfold as well as his role as legitimate leader of the sheep (10:1-2, 5). He is the one who may enter through the door, and his right to do so is recognized by the doorkeeper who lets him in (10:3). But it is the sheep themselves who are the most important evidence of his right of entry, for they hear his voice, recognize him, and follow him out. He leads them out and goes before them (10:3–5). Their recognition of him and his voice implies a prior relationship.

There is unanimous agreement among scholars that it is Jesus to whom the figure of the shepherd points. This unanimity—a relatively rare occurrence in Johannine studies—may be attributed directly to the unequivocal message of the implied author, conveyed to us readers through the mouth of the Johannine Jesus, who declares, "I am the good shepherd" (10:11, 14). That Jesus is reliable in this identification is supported by the fact that all details of the shepherd's portrayal in chapter 10 are consistent with the characterization of Jesus throughout the gospel, particularly in the cosmological tale.

Furthermore, all of the descriptions of the good shepherd in 10:7–18 are phrased in language which has its context in the cosmological tale. For example, the assertion in 10:10 "I came that they may have life, and have it abundantly," echoes the many other passages, such as 3:16 and 5:24, in which eternal life and indeed resurrection are promised to those who believe. The readiness of the good shepherd to lay down his life for the sheep in order to take it up again (10:11, 14b, 17–18) is said repeatedly of Jesus throughout the gospel (e.g., 16:28 and 17:11, 13). The same is true of the mutual knowledge between the shepherd and his sheep, which parallels that between the Father and Jesus (10:14, cf. 17:25; 14:20). Finally, the shepherd's mission to bring also "other sheep, that are not of this fold" (10:16) is similar to Jesus' prophecy in 12:32, "and I, when I am lifted up from the earth, will draw all people to myself."[1] The Johannine Jesus therefore leaves no doubt that he is the shepherd of the *paroimia*.

The Sheep. The identification of the sheep is also clear, though perhaps more complicated than that of the shepherd. Verses 10:1–5 define them primarily in relationship to the shepherd on the one hand and the thief on the other. In addition, the sheep bear a spatial relationship to the fold. They are in the fold when the shepherd comes. They hear the shepherd's voice, and his own (τὰ ἴδια) follow him out of the fold (10:3, 4) but do not heed, recognize, or follow the thief (10:5, 8). Finally, the sheep are benefited by the actions of the shepherd but potentially harmed by those of the thief (10:10) and, according to 10:12, by those of the hireling and wolf as well. The sheep therefore symbolize humankind, often referred to metaphorically as the "world" in this gospel.[2]

---

[1] That 12:32 refers to the Gentile mission is suggested by its context. Jesus' comment can be read as part of his response to the desire of the Gentiles to see him (cf. 12:20). Here, as in 7:35, the mission to the Gentiles must begin after Jesus' departure from the world. The identification of the Gentiles in this chapter as Greek or Diaspora Jews, however, has been argued by H. B. Kossen, "Who were the Greeks of John XII 20?," *Studies in John: J. N. Sevenster Festschrift* (Leiden: Brill, 1970) 97–110.

[2] See pages 38–41 above.

The use of the word "his own" in 10:3, 4 implies a distinction between a general group of people who heard Jesus—the sheep—and those specific individuals whom he called by name and led out of the sheepfold.[3] If so, the latter group may be identified with some confidence as those who believe in Jesus. It is they who are called by name (cf. 1:42), hear and heed Jesus' voice (cf. 5:24–25), follow him out of the sheepfold (10:3–4; cf. 1:43; 21:19, 22), and are promised abundant and eternal life (10:10, 28; 5:24). It is the believers' well-being which is threatened by the forces opposed to Jesus (16:2; 17:15). This threat, however, is only potential. As long as the sheep refuse to recognize and follow the stranger, as long as they remain under the protection of the shepherd and not some hireling, the thief and wolf will have no power and their destructive aims will be thwarted. Similarly, the believers are protected and guarded, by both Jesus and the Father (17:12; 10:29). Finally, to this group will in the future be added other sheep "not of this fold" (10:16). The future participation of this group, usually identified as Gentile believers in Christ,[4] will create a much desired situation in which there will be "one flock, one shepherd" (10:16).

Again, the parallels between the *paroimia* and the cosmological tale are clear. Just as his own sheep in 10:1–5 hear the shepherd's voice and follow him out of the fold, so do the human beings who truly hear Jesus follow him, both in the sense of obeying Jesus and also in the sense of following him out of the world. His own sheep, who heed the shepherd and follow him out of the fold, are those who "received him" and have "believed in his name" (1:12; cf. 20:31).

The Sheepfold. If the "sheep" correspond to the metaphorical use of κόσμος as humankind in the Fourth Gospel, the fold parallels the spatial dimension of this term. Whatever its precise size and architectural features,[5] the sheepfold is an enclosure, though not an impenetrable one. As such, it serves to keep the sheep in and most others out. It therefore protects the sheep from unlawful intruders until the coming of their shepherd, but it also restricts their freedom of movement. In the *paroimia* one gains rightful access to the fold by means of a door or gate (10:1, 2) over which a gatekeeper (10:3) presides.

---

[3] In the *paroimia* itself nothing is made of the possibility that some sheep of this fold will be left behind, though this is implied by 10:26.

[4] For example, AB 1.396; Haenchen, *John 2,* 49; Simonis, 297–301. Martyn (*Christian History,* 117–21), however, revives the suggestion made by Schoeps and others that these "other sheep" may in fact refer to "Jewish Christians belonging to conventicles known to but separate from the Johannine community." See R. E. Brown, "Other Sheep Not of This Fold: The Johannine Perspective on Christian Diversity in the Late First Century," *JBL* 97 (1978) 5–22; H. J. Schoeps, *Jewish Christianity* (Philadelphia: Fortress, 1969).

[5] See Quasten, 6, and AB 1.385, for their brief descriptions of the physical sheepfold evoked by the passage.

In order to take care of his sheep, the shepherd must enter the fold to gather his flock and then leave the fold again. Therefore by definition his point of origin is outside the fold, though the exact location is not specified. He enters it and then leaves again. In looking at the relationship between the shepherd and the sheepfold, we may therefore discern a three-step pattern of movement: the shepherd begins outside the fold, enters into the fold and engages in some activity pertaining to the sheep, and exits from the fold, returning to his starting position outside it.

It is now necessary to determine the meaning of this pattern within the context of the gospel. This involves an assumption that the pattern of movement in the *paroimia* is paralleled by the activity of Jesus—the shepherd—within the gospel narrative as a whole. As we have seen in our survey of Johannine scholarship, the assumption that parallels between the *paroimia* and other aspects of the Johannine narrative exist is one of the constants of the various interpretations of this passage. But this assumption has not been applied in detail with respect to the relationship between the shepherd and the sheepfold as it has with respect to the animate elements of the passage, such as the sheep and the thief/bandit. It may be suggested, however, that it is in fact the shepherd's activity vis-à-vis the fold which defines the relationship of the other elements to one another.

The three-step pattern of movement of the shepherd calls to mind the general structure of the cosmological tale. In this tale, Jesus is portrayed as originating from the Father—temporally and spatially outside the realm of the created world—becoming flesh and "tabernacling" (cf. 1:14: ἐσκήνωσεν) in the world, and then, upon completion of his mission, departing out of the world again. It is this parallel pattern which suggests that it is the world as a spatial entity or enclosure in which human beings (sheep) find themselves, which is represented by the sheepfold.

Like the shepherd, Jesus approaches the main arena of his activity from a point outside it. But this is known only by the readers and, to some extent, the disciples, who are privy to the cosmological tale.[6] After entering the sheepfold, the shepherd engages in activities which are described in the *paroimia* as calling his own sheep by name and leading them out of the sheepfold (10:3). This

---

[6] Within the historical tale, Jesus is perceived by the Jewish audience concerned with his identity as being one of their number, from Galilee (7:41), whose parents are known to them (6:42). Jesus challenges them to correct their false understanding by revealing to them his origins as detailed in the cosmological tale: "You know me, and you know where I come from? But I have not come of my own accord; he who sent me is true, and him you do not know" (7:28). This challenge, though falling on the deaf ears of Jesus' immediate audience, is intended, one presumes, to be picked up by the implied readers.

calling is in effect a gathering together of his own, in preparation for their departure from the sheepfold.

This description is strongly reminiscent of the activity of Jesus which may be described in general terms as gathering disciples. In the Johannine description of the call of the first disciples, Jesus' calling them by name plays a significant role. On his first encounter with Peter, Jesus comments, "You are Simon, son of John. You are to be called Cephas" (1:42). As he watched Nathanael approaching him, Jesus describes him as "truly an Israelite, in whom there is no deceit" (1:47), a comment which Nathanael sees as indicative of Jesus' prior knowledge of him (1:48).[7] Therefore this passage describes Jesus as calling his own, now followers and disciples, by name.

The theme of gathering of disciples is prominent throughout the Johannine narrative and is highlighted, for example, in the episode with the Samaritan woman, which results in the allegiance of the Samaritans (4:42). The theme is also referred to explicitly later in chapter 4, when the disciples are enjoined to "reap" and "gather fruit" (4:36), and perhaps also in chapter 15, in which they are exhorted to "bear fruit" (15:1–4).[8] Jesus' prayer in chapter 17 also presupposes that the disciples will continue this aspect of Jesus' activity with some success. He prays not only for the disciples he has sent into the world (17:18) but "also on behalf of those who will believe in me through their word" (17:20). That this activity continues until the moment of his departure, or ascension, is symbolized by Jesus' encounter with Mary Magdalene, in which he calls her by name, thereby revealing his identity to her (20:16).

The shepherd gathers together his sheep in order to lead them out of the sheepfold (10:4). Although the fold is not explicitly described in negative terms, the shepherd's leading his sheep out implies that leaving the fold is a positive act, leading to the sustenance of the sheep, just as leaving the world is essential for the salvation and eternal life of the believers. This parallel is reinforced by the subsequent discourse (10:7ff.), which speaks of the shepherd as "saving" the sheep (10:9) and providing them with abundant (10:9) and eternal life (10:28). These, of course, are the same benefits which Jesus provides for his own, that is, those who believe in him (3:16–18).

After the shepherd has gathered all his own, he leaves ($\pi o\rho\epsilon\acute{u}\epsilon\tau\alpha\iota$) the sheepfold and leads the sheep out as well. The shepherd's departure from the fold

---

[7] It is also important that the believers know Jesus' name, a knowledge manifested through the appropriate use of christological titles (cf. 11:27; 20:28).

[8] For detailed discussion of 15:1–6, see AB 2.668–679, in which Brown sees the bearing of fruit as symbolic both of possessing divine life and of spreading it to others. In a different way, this theme is present also in the bread of life discourse, as a result of which many disciples leave, though not the Twelve (6:66–69).

is paralleled within the cosmological tale with Jesus' departure from the world, which comes to the fore in the latter part of the gospel, beginning in chapter 12, and is the central theme of the Farewell Discourses. In 13:1, the narrator refers to Jesus' knowledge that the time had come to depart out of the world, and in the discourses Jesus speaks openly of going to the Father (πορεύομαι: 14:12, 28; ὑπάγω 16:5; πορευθῶ: 16:7; ἔρχομαι: 17:11, 13) and even of ascending to the Father (20:17), from whom he had been sent into the world (17:5). This departure marks the completion of the three-step pattern of the shepherd's activity, which we have discerned both in the *paroimia* and in the cosmological tale within the gospel narrative as a whole. This pattern is summarized aptly in 16:28: "I came from the Father and have come into the world; again, I am leaving the world and am going to [πορεύομαι] the Father."

In the *paroimia*, as in the cosmological tale, the departure of the shepherd from the fold is a prelude to the departure of his sheep. As we have seen, the shepherd departs from the fold at the head of his flock, who follow him out (10:4). Similarly, Jesus' departure from the world, which also marks his return to the Father, is, or perhaps will be, followed by the departure of those who believe in him.

This act of following is usually understood literally, as referring to shepherding practices in ancient Palestine, in which the shepherd walked at the head of his flock.[9] But the act of following has both spatial and temporal dimensions and can be understood in both a literal and figurative sense. The Johannine use of the verb ἀκολουθέω does sometimes emphasize its spatial aspect, as in 1:37, 38, and 40, which describe two of the disciples of John the Baptist as walking behind Jesus. The fact that the spatial connotations of this verb are almost always associated with the disciples implies that they also refer figuratively to the state of discipleship itself. This figurative meaning is underscored by the thrice-repeated command: "Follow me!" which the Johannine Jesus addresses to Philip in 1:43 and to Simon Peter in 21:19,22.

Although ἀκολουθέω implies an ongoing, continuous activity, it would seem that eventually the followers actually arrive at their destination: "Whoever serves me must follow me, and where I am, there will my servant be also" (12:26). John 10:27–28 specifies this goal: "My sheep...follow me. I give them eternal life..." This is also implied in 8:12, in which Jesus says: "I am the light of the world; whoever follows me will never walk in darkness but will have the light of life." Therefore following Jesus, like believing in him, results in eternal

---

[9] Rihbany (*The Syrian Christ*, 212), who tries to explicate the life and teachings of Jesus against the background of life in the Middle East, cautions us that we must not see this practice as invariable: "As a rule, the shepherd goes before the flock, but not infrequently he is seen behind it" (emphasis is Rihbany's).

life. In the latter two references, the spatial aspect of the act of following gives way to the temporal aspect: by definition, the followers arrive at their goal some time after their leader does.[10] The temporal connotations of ἀκολουθέω are explicit in 13:36, in which Jesus tells Simon Peter: "Where I am going, you cannot follow me now; but you will follow afterward." This is explained more fully in Jesus' promise to his disciples in 14:2–3: "In my Father's house there are many dwelling places; if it were not so, would I have told you that I go to prepare a place for you? And if I go and prepare a place for you, I will come again and will take you to myself, so that where I am you may be also."

Those who believe in Jesus, therefore, will follow him, not only literally, by walking with or behind him, or figuratively, by obeying him and being his disciples, but also, if one may say so, soteriologically, by being resurrected from the dead and ascending to the Father. The "shepherd" therefore goes before the "sheep" not only as master, but also as their guide into his Father's realm. In 10:4, the emphasis is not on the delay between the return of Jesus and the departure of the "sheep" from the fold but on Jesus' leadership—he blazes the trail, as it were; where he goes, his sheep will follow.

The activity of the shepherd with respect to the sheepfold in the *paroimia* therefore parallels that of Jesus with respect to the world in the cosmological tale of the gospel narrative. In both cases, the protagonist enters the enclosure from outside, gathers his own, and then exits, followed by those who belong to him.

These parallels imply that one should identify the sheepfold not primarily with the Jewish theocracy, as it must be within the historical tale, but with the "world" as understood within the cosmological tale. Although, as we have already noted, the word κόσμος can sometimes refer generally to humankind, or specifically to those people who reject the Word, that is, the Jews (cf. 1:10), this does not appear to be the dominant sense in the *paroimia*. The main reason for this is that the Jews are parallel not to the fold from which Jesus' own must depart, but to those sheep who are not his own, since in 10:26 Jesus chastises them for not belonging to his sheep. Instead, the sheepfold in the *paroimia* is to be identified with the κόσμος as a negative spatial entity associated with death and darkness, from which the sheep—human beings—must depart in order to gain salvation. While unbelieving Jews inhabit this negative spatial entity and by failing to believe are unable to leave it behind, the κόσμος here is not itself associated with Judaism, the Jewish theocracy, or specific Jewish institutions. Unlike Paul's letters to the Romans and the Galatians, the Fourth Gospel does

---

[10] Cf. Hoskyns, *Fourth Gospel*, 372; Nicholson, *Death as Departure*, 114.

not explicitly see Jewish institutions and practices as hindrances to faith in Christ.[11]

The Gate. No discussion of the sheepfold is complete without considering its auxiliary elements, the gate and the gatekeeper. Just as the predominant understanding of the fold as Judaism, the Jewish theocracy, or the temple implies, at least for some scholars, a specific content for these two elements, so it is for the interpretation being offered here.

Gates or doors by their very nature are ambivalent things. As part of an enclosed space such as a building, they mark the threshold between one room and another; outside, they close off passageways connecting one property with another. Open doors allow free passage from one realm to another; closed doors can keep one in, either in safety or in captivity, or keep one out, either to one's relief or one's dismay.

In the *paroimia,* the gate is the threshold between the sheepfold and the area outside it. That the implied author, through the mouth of the Johannine Jesus, attaches symbolic significance to the gate is indicated by the fact that the Johannine Jesus identifies himself as such in 10:7 and 9. These verses, their meaning, their relationship to each other as well as to the *paroimia* in 10:1–5 are, as we have noted, the focus of considerable scholarly attention. The initial problem is the apparent inconsistency between Jesus as the gate in 10:7 and 9 and his identification as shepherd in 10:11ff. Apparently, ancient scribes were troubled by this discrepancy as well, since in some texts, such as p75 and the Sahidic version, 10:7 reads "shepherd" instead of "gate".

Scholars agree that "gate," as the more difficult reading, is to be preferred.[12] As an expression of Johannine theology, however, the image of Jesus as gate is consistent with other christological formulations within the gospel narrative which depict Jesus as the sole point through which the believers can gain access to God and hence to salvation (cf. 1:14–18). The image is reminiscent of 14:6, in which Jesus tells his disciples, "I am the way and the truth and the life. No one comes to the Father except through me."

The simultaneous definition of Jesus as both gate and shepherd presents logistical difficulties when applied to 10:1–5, causing most scholars to favor the interpretation of Jesus as shepherd when it comes to the exegesis of the *paroimia.*

---

[11] This is the case despite the presence of the theme that Jesus replaces the institutions of Judaism, a theme which has often been noted, for example, in 2:1–11, 13–22, in 4:21, 23 and elsewhere in the gospel. But in these passages, the Johannine Jesus is not leading his followers away from these institutions, but rather making a christological declaration that the purpose of these institutions will henceforth be fulfilled in him. For discussion, see the major commentaries on these verses, especially AB 1 and 2.

[12] See AB 1.386, Schnack. 2.288, and Quasten, 158.

Within the *paroimia*, the gate has two functions. First, it is the way through which the legitimate shepherd gains entry to the sheepfold and thereby also access to the sheep. It is also the means through which the shepherd, as well as the sheep, leave the sheepfold. In the *paroimia* the gate is therefore integrally related to the process of salvation: those who enter lead others to salvation, and the sheep who exit will be saved. This connection has of course not been lost on scholars, who connect this image with Ps 118:19–20: "Open to me the gates of righteousness, that I may enter through them and give thanks to the Lord. This is the gate of the Lord; the righteous shall enter through it."[13]

If we see the *paroimia* as a symbolic reference to the cosmological tale, in which the sheepfold is the world, then it would appear that it is the incarnation by which Jesus enters the world, and it is the Passion, including the crucifixion, resurrection, and ascension, by which he leaves it. These events therefore are the means by which Jesus crosses the threshold between this world and the realm of the Father.

Although the incarnation is referred to directly only in 1:14, it is implied in Johannine descriptions of Jesus as the bread of life (6:48) and the true light (1:9; cf. 8:12), which has descended from heaven (6:51) and come into the world (1:9). The incarnation would seem to be the corollary of the Father's decision to send his Son into the world. Similarly, Jesus' death and resurrection are referred to frequently as the means by which he departs from the world and returns to the Father (16:20,28). It is also the event which provides a model for and reassurance of the eternal life of the believers. That is, Jesus' christological claims are authenticated by his resurrection and ascension; therefore the promises which he has made to the believers are, or will be, fulfilled. They have experienced now, and/or will experience in the future, the resurrection and eternal life, as Jesus has. Similarly, Jesus' followers enter the "sheepfold" at birth. They leave figuratively or spiritually by following or believing in Jesus, with the result that they are in the world but not of the world (15:19). They then literally or physically leave the world at his return.

In 10:9, the gate functions somewhat differently than in the *paroimia*. As in 10:1–5, it is the threshold which marks the boundary between condemnation and salvation. In 10:9, as in 10:7, however, the gate is explicitly identified as Jesus. Whereas in 10:1–5 the area linked with condemnation is the fold, as the world without the presence of Jesus, in 10:9 it is the space outside the fold which is the locus of condemnation. Whereas in 10:1–5 it is the departure from the sheepfold that is linked to the sheep's salvation, in 10:9 it is their entry through

---

[13] Schnack. 2.290; AB 1.394; Adolf Schlatter, *Der Evangelist Johannes* (3rd ed.; Stuttgart: Calwer Verlag, 1960) 235. These verses have led some to identify the gate as the gate to the temple, which is open only to the just (cf. John 5:2; Acts 3:2).

the gate that effects salvation ("Whoever enters by me will be saved"). Furthermore, 10:9 defines the saved sheep as those who "will come in and go out and find pasture," whereas 10:1–5 focuses solely on their departure.

Noting the discrepancies between 10:9 and 10:1–5, Schnackenburg warns that "we should not press the image too closely....The only thing that matters is the end in view: to reach the pasture of life."[14] This warning is well-taken. It is noteworthy, however, that the pattern of movement attributed to the saved sheep in 10:9 is the same as that associated with the shepherd in 10:1–5: they enter by the gate, and then they exit in order to enjoy the necessities of life, that is, pasture. While this formulation may simply imply freedom of movement, as Schnackenburg states,[15] it is possible to understand this pattern of movement according to the cosmological tale. The entry of the sheep through the gate may be understood as their birth from above (3:7). This spiritual rebirth marks their entry into the Kingdom of God as expressed in the world, namely, the community of believers.[16] Their sojourn within the fold, which, though unmentioned in 10:9 is implied as the location into which the gate provides entry and from which the sheep leave for pasture, is their earthly life within this community. Their departure for pasture is their physical death and their enjoyment of eternal life. Such an interpretation, though somewhat speculative, would be compatible with the thread of realized eschatology which runs through the gospel narrative.[17]

The Gatekeeper. If the plain meaning of the "gate" is relatively easy to extrapolate from a cosmological reading of the *paroimia*, the same is not true for the gatekeeper. Virtually all scholars who attempt an interpretation of the *paroimia* seem to experience mild despair at the task of identifying the gatekeeper with a character within, or for that matter, outside of, the gospel narrative. St. Augustine commented on this problem by noting that the Johannine Jesus has explained much of the passage, but has "left us to search out the doorkeeper for ourselves." Although Augustine himself believed that the doorkeeper, like the door and the shepherd, is Jesus himself, he suggested that an appropriate solution to the problem is to "let each one make the choice that pleases him, but let him

---

[14] Schnack. 2.293.

[15] Ibid.

[16] Or the Johannine community, in the ecclesiological tale.

[17] Some scholars, such as Bultmann (377, n. 6), see 10:9 as an allusion to Num 27:17, in which Moses refers to a leader "who shall go out before them and come in before them, who shall lead them out and bring them in; so that the congregation of the Lord may not be like sheep without a shepherd." It must be noted, however, that the direction of movement in Num 27:17 is directly contrary to that in John 10:9, in which the sheep "come in and go out." If John 10:9 is in fact an allusion to Num 27:17, then the reversal of the pattern of movement may support the cosmological interpretation we have suggested .

think of it reverently."[18] Some of the specific suggestions that have been made include Moses,[19] God,[20] the Holy Spirit,[21] Caiaphas,[22] and John the Baptist.[23] Scholars who see the *paroimia* as a parable often find no place for the gatekeeper in their interpretation at all. For example, Schnackenburg declares that he is a secondary figure who has little significance for the meaning of the passage.[24] Rudolf Bultmann mentions him only in a footnote, cautioning the reader not to give him undue importance.[25]

Within the historical tale, it is difficult, if not impossible, to find a character who fits this description. The result is that scholars often do not identify him at all, ascribing his presence in the *paroimia* to a desire on the part of Jesus, or the evangelist, to lend verisimilitude to the pastoral scene.[26]

Within the cosmological tale, however, there is a figure who qualifies, though with some limitations. As with the "gate" image, the definition of the gatekeeper is dependent on our interpretation of the sheepfold. His role within the *paroimia* is to stand at the entrance to the fold. It is he who opens the door to allow the legitimate shepherd to enter, and also, presumably, to allow him to leave again with his flock. Because of this function, he has been defined by some scholars as the criterion or judge of the identity of the true shepherd, whence the attempts to define him as God.[27] In John 1 and 3, it is John the Baptist who serves a similar function with respect to Jesus. John the Baptist has been suggested as a candidate for the role of gatekeeper by some older exegetes, such as Godet, who argues that "it was indeed [John the Baptist]...whom Jesus had in mind [as author of the *paroimia*]; for it was he whom God raised up in Israel for the express purpose of announcing the Messiah, and introducing Him into the theocracy."[28]

Although Godet situates John the Baptist primarily within the historical tale, his comment points to the fact that John the Baptist plays an important

[18] Augustine, *Lectures or Tractates on the Gospel According to John,* vol. 2, in *The Works of Aurelius Augustine* (ed. Marcus Dods, trans. James Innes; Edinburgh: T. and T. Clark, 1874) 11.91.

[19] John Chrysostom, *Homilies on the Gospel of St. John,* 59.3, in *Nicene and Post-Nicene Fathers,* (Grand Rapids: Eerdmans, 1956) 14.214.

[20] Schlatter, *Johannes,* 234.

[21] Quasten (10) cites Cornelius a Lapide, *Commentaria in Quattuor Evangelia* (Augustae Taurinorum, 1899) as representing this viewpoint.

[22] Simonis, 154–59, esp. 158.

[23] Godet, 381.

[24] Schnack. 2.282.

[25] Bultmann, 372, note 2.

[26] E.g., Quasten, 51.

[27] Robinson ("Parable," 236) contends that the gatekeeper served this function in the original parables which underlie the *paroimia*.

[28] Godet, 381.

role in the cosmological tale as well. Like Jesus, the Baptist was sent by God. He was sent for the express purpose of testifying or bearing witness to the light who was coming into the world (1:7), thereby revealing his presence to Israel. Hence John was present in the world before Jesus, just as the gatekeeper is present in, or at the entrance to, the fold before the shepherd comes.

The Baptist begins to function as witness in 1:26–27, in which he informs the Jews who have been interrogating him that he is merely the forerunner of the one whom they appear to be seeking. But it is only in 1:29–34 that he, in a formal and detailed way, announces the presence of Jesus in the world. Although this announcement is directed initially toward the representatives of the Jewish establishment (1:19), it is clear that Jesus' arrival has implications not only for Israel, but for the world, as 1:29 indicates.[29] Seeing Jesus coming towards him,[30] John announces, "Here is the lamb of God who takes away the sin of the world!" (1:29). This announcement emphasizes Jesus' divine connections and places his role in a universal context. The ability of John the Baptist to recognize Jesus and to judge him to be the one whom he was sent to announce was given to him by God. It was God who verified Jesus' identity as the Son of God by allowing the Baptist to witness the Spirit descending on Jesus and remaining there (1:32–34).

Finally, it is the Baptist who gives Jesus his first two "sheep." By identifying Jesus as the Lamb of God in the presence of two of his disciples, John the Baptist encourages them to follow Jesus (1:35–39). The Baptist's "flock" diminishes even as that of Jesus increases, a situation which is troubling to some of John's disciples but looked upon favorably by the Baptist himself. This is expressed in language which is strongly reminiscent of our *paroimia:*

> He who has the bride is the bridegroom. The friend of the bridegroom, who stands and *hears* him, rejoices greatly at the bridegroom's *voice.* For this reason my joy has been fulfilled. He must increase, but I must decrease (3:29–30; emphasis mine).[31]

It is true that the Baptist, perhaps unlike the gatekeeper of the *paroimia*, is not directly responsible for the shepherd's entry into the fold, that is, Jesus'

---

[29] This is indicated not only by 1:29 but also by 1:10, in which the term κόσμος, repeated three times, refers not only to the physical world, but also to Israel, the Jewish people, who "knew him not."

[30] The present participle ἐρχόμενος appears in the almost formulaic descriptions of Jesus in 4:25 ("...the Christ, he who is coming into the world") and 6:14 ("the prophet who is coming into the world").

[31] This detail might explain why it is that the Baptist is not portrayed as a disciple of Jesus. Though he too hears Jesus' voice and rejoices at his appearance, his function is to let him into the fold and release his (temporary) charges to him, but not to follow him himself.

incarnation. He does serve, however, both to "open the door" to the shepherd, by making known his presence in the world, and to turn the care of the sheep over to him. This he does by being witness to the christological identity of Jesus and verifying his central role in the cosmological tale.

The Thief. The last element—though by no means the least important—which must be accounted for is the thief/bandit/stranger, the references to whom begin and conclude the *paroimia*.[32] Within 10:1–5 this figure is contrasted with the shepherd with respect to the mode of entry into the sheepfold as well as the response on the part of the sheep. Whereas the shepherd enters by the door and is known and followed by the sheep, the thief/bandit enters "another way," by stealth, and his presence is ignored by the sheep since they do not know him or recognize his voice. Because of the centrality of this figure to the *paroimia*, we will look carefully at the views of others and make our own attempts at identifying him.

As with the gatekeeper, there have been several candidates proposed for the role of thief/bandit in this passage. Some scholars find their "thief" in the post–biblical Jewish or early Christian tradition which formed part of the background to the gospel. For example, Wellhausen[33] and Bernard[34] identified the thieves and robbers as false messiahs, similar to the ones against whom the Synoptic Jesus warns his audience (Mark 13:5, 22 and parallels). Along different lines, Zahn suggests that Jesus' opponents here are the bad priests and kings of the Hasmonean and Herodian dynasties respectively, both of which "came before" Jesus (cf. 10:8).[35] Hoskyns defines the thief as the antichrists who deny the authority of the historical Jesus,[36] while Simonis sets the entire passage against the background of zealot nationalism in first-century Palestine.[37]

The majority of scholars, however, search the gospel narrative itself and identify the thief with the Jewish leadership of the time of Jesus, whose opposition to Jesus is reflected in the historical tale within the Johannine narrative.[38] Haenchen speaks of the high priests and Pharisees whose tenure as officials in Jerusalem antedates the time of the evangelist, hence making sense of Jesus' comment in 10:8, that "all who came before me are thieves and bandits."[39]

---

[32] Though these three terms are used, the figures they denote perform the same function in the *paroimia* and therefore are to be taken as a single narrative character.

[33] Wellhausen, *Das Evangelium Johannis*, 47.

[34] Bernard, *Commentary*, 346.

[35] T. Zahn, *Das Evangelium des Johannes Ausgelegt* (Leipzig: A. Deichert, 1908) 444.

[36] Hoskyns, *The Fourth Gospel*, 368.

[37] Simonis, 210–14.

[38] Culpepper, 86–98.

[39] Haenchen, *John 2*, 47.

Brown would include the Sadducees along with the Pharisees in this category.[40] These and most other recent scholars agree with the judgment of John Quasten, that in chapter 10, "the Pharisees, who regard themselves as the real leaders of the people, are branded as false leaders and as guides to error."[41]

As we have already noted, one of the principal arguments offered in favor of this position is the perceived relationship between chapters 9 and 10. The man born blind, whose healing is described in chapter 9, is seen as an example of a "sheep" who follows and believes in Jesus (9:38). The shepherd is of course Jesus himself, and the Pharisees (9:13) or Jews (9:18), who seem to be interchangeable in chapter 9, are the thieves and robbers of chapter 10. In other words, the contrast between the shepherd and thief of 10:1–5 is considered to parallel that between Jesus and the Jewish leadership as portrayed in chapter 9, and indeed throughout the gospel as a whole. In order to assess this viewpoint, it is necessary to look at what information is provided by the *paroimia* as well as by the discourse which follows it.

In 10:1–5, the thief attempts to enter the sheepfold, presumably in order to steal the sheep. He does not enter through the gate, however, but climbs in another way. This stealthy entry is contrasted with that of the shepherd and serves to emphasize the illegitimacy of the thief's presence in the sheepfold and of his claim to the sheep. Once in, he presumably tries to coax the sheep out of the sheepfold, but they refuse to follow him, since he is a stranger whose voice they do not recognize (10:5). The *paroimia* therefore implies that the focal point of the contrast between the thief and the shepherd is the issue of authority, an authority which does not emerge from among the sheep but comes from outside the sheepfold. The language of the *paroimia* of course labels the shepherd—Jesus—as the legitimate authority, an identification corroborated by the doorkeeper[42] and the sheep themselves. Therefore the passage portrays the thief

---

[40] In this way Brown (AB 1.392) takes into account the possibility that the verse may also allude to the evil rulers of the Hasmonean period.

[41] Quasten, 153. The fact that λῃστής is used to describe Barabbas in 18:40 is not, in my view, particularly helpful in elucidating the meaning of the term in 10:1. This judgment is based upon the fact that it is difficult to connect Barabbas, about whom we are told very little in this gospel, to the shepherd's—i.e., Jesus'—opposition, which is the role of the λῃστής in the *paroimia*. A different position is held by Simonis (131–32), for whom 18:40 is an important starting point. Simonis views λῃστής as designating not robber or bandit, but rather zealot, as it does in Josephus. This is important for his allegorical interpretation of the *paroimia* against the backdrop of political events in Judea before the first Jewish revolt. It must be noted, however, that such a reading does not emerge from the intrinsic data provided by the gospel itself.

[42] Some scholars view the "door" and "doorkeeper" images as the criterion which distinguishes between the good shepherd and the thief. See Schlatter, *Johannes,* 233; Paul W. Meyer, "A Note on John 10:1–18," *JBL* 75 (1956) 233. For a different analysis, see Adele

as attempting to exert his influence, for some unspecified, but presumably evil purpose, over someone else's sheep.

The image of the thief and bandit is elaborated upon in the interpretation which the Johannine Jesus himself provides for the *paroimia*. In 10:8 Jesus declares that "All who came before me are thieves and robbers; but the sheep did not heed them." In contrast to 10:1 and 10:10, this verse refers not to one figure but many, as indicated by the plural forms κλέπται...καὶ λησταί, and even more emphatically by πάντες ("all"). This contradiction can be resolved by reading the singular "thief" of 10:1 as a collective noun and as paradigmatic for the behavior of all such threatening figures. More problematic, however, is the temporal relationship which the verse implies. John 10:8a brands all who came (ἦλθον—aorist indicative) before Jesus as robbers and thieves, i.e., as attempting—albeit unsuccessfully—to exert harmful control over his sheep. But if the latter are the believers in Jesus, then strictly speaking there could have been no such flock before Jesus came and hence no believers to heed (ἤκουσαν—also aorist indicative) these interlopers. This problem is generally solved by considering the aorist indicative ἦλθον to mean that "all who came before Jesus" were still present and active after Jesus' arrival, at which time the sheep, who recognized and followed their shepherd, did not heed the thieves. In this way the "all" who are thieves and robbers can still be taken to refer to the Jewish authorities.[43] This solution would be more attractive, however, if ἤκουσαν were in the present tense, as are the verbs in 10:1–5 (cf. especially 10:3: ἀκούει).

Verse 10:10 is more straightforward, describing the evil intentions of the thief and robber. He comes in order to steal, kill, and destroy the sheep (10:10a); Jesus, in contrast, came in order to give life in abundance (10:10b). The consequence of following the thief is death; the benefit of following the shepherd is life. In the Johannine context, of course, the terms "death" and "life" do not refer primarily to physical existence, but to the eternal fate of the "sheep" or humanity. Eternal life is salvation; death is condemnation (cf. 8:21). This suggests that in order to steal, kill, and destroy the sheep, i.e., lead them to their death, the thief, or the wolf, must drive the sheep away from their belief in Jesus.

Reinhartz, "The Shepherd and the Sheep: John 10:1–5 Reconsidered," *Proceedings of the Eastern Great Lakes Biblical Society* 9 (1989) 161–77.

[43] Schnack. (2.291) cautions against considering personages from salvation history, such as the prophets and kings, or John the Baptist, to be the referents here because they are men of God and witnesses to Jesus. He suggests that we see 10:8 as a broad and general reference to all Jewish opponents of Jesus' time.

At this point in the discourse, the thief gives way to two other figures.[44] The first, and more prominent, is the hireling. Like the thief and robber in 10:1–5, he is described in explicit contrast with the shepherd. Like the thief, he is not the owner of the sheep, nor does he care for them: he flees from the wolf, placing his own welfare above that of the sheep. The second figure is the wolf, who snatches and scatters the sheep, resulting in the destruction of the flock and probably the death of the individual sheep as well. He is not contrasted explicitly with the shepherd, though it is clear that he poses a threat similar to that of the thief.

What are we to make of these two figures in the context of the chapter as a whole? Are the hireling, the wolf, and the thief simply three ways of describing the same source of opposition to Jesus, or does each have a different referent?[45] Some have suggested that both the hireling and the thief refer to the Jews and Pharisees, whereas the wolf is just a wolf, a detail which evokes the pastoral setting while highlighting the inadequacy of the hireling.[46] Others have argued that neither the hireling nor the wolf should be identified with specific figures in the gospel or indeed outside of it.[47] There is another possibility, however. From the point of view of the sheep, and indeed of the shepherd as well, it is the thief and the wolf who play a similar role.[48] They both aim to destroy the flock, whereas the hireling is merely uncaring. Although his actions put the flock at risk, their destruction is the consequence but not the aim of his behavior.

Taking into account 10:1–18 as a whole, our thief therefore has three salient characteristics: he, or perhaps they, preceded Jesus (10:8); he claims to have, and tries to assert, power and control over the believers (10:5); and he aims to kill them (10:10), which in the Johannine context can only be accomplished by forcing them away from their faith in Jesus.

The Jewish authorities, the logical candidates for the role of thief within the historical tale, seem to fill the bill in some respects. Certainly the Pharisees, high priests, and other figures were "rulers of the Jews" (cf. 3:1) before Jesus came into the world. Second, they are clearly portrayed within the Johannine narrative as authority figures who attempt to control the Jews, from whose ranks Jesus' followers have come. From their own perspective, of course, the Jewish

---

[44] Brown (AB 1.395) suggests that at this point the redactor has made use of a new parable of Jesus.

[45] E. Schwartz ("Osterbetrachtungen," *ZNW* 7 (1906) 5, n.1) identifies the thief with Herod and his dynasty, the hireling as the High Priest and the wolf as Rome. For a discussion of the wolf as Rome, see Simonis, 285–88.

[46] Hoskyns (*The Fourth Gospel*, 377) identifies the hireling with the thief, but does not provide a referent for the wolf.

[47] Schnack. 2.296. For a summary of the various views, see Simonis, 278–80.

[48] This is argued also by Godet (387, 392) who suggests that the hirelings are the priests and the Levites, while the wolf and the thieves are the Pharisees.

authorities are not thieves or false leaders at all. Rather, they are the legitimate political and religious authorities over their compatriots. This is stated explicitly in 7:26, in which the Jewish crowds refer to the "authorities," and in 3:1, in which Nicodemus is described by the narrator as a "leader of the Jews." These authorities have control over others whom they can delegate to accomplish certain tasks. They send priests and Levites to interrogate John the Baptist (1:19ff.) and order their officers to arrest Jesus (7:32). They also criticize for their legal transgressions those whom they perceive to be under their jurisdiction. For example, the lame man is admonished for carrying his pallet on the Sabbath (5:10); Jesus is persecuted and eventually prosecuted for blasphemy (10:33; 5:17) as well as for his transgressions of the Sabbath laws (5:16, 18).

That the Jewish authorities feel threatened by Jesus' activity is evident in their dismay at his success. In 11:48, the Pharisees lament that if everyone believes in him, "the Romans will come and destroy both our holy place and our nation." To avoid this situation, suggests Caiaphas the high priest, it is expedient to kill Jesus (11:50). In 12:19, the Pharisees apparently concede defeat, saying to one another: "You see, you can do nothing. Look, the world has gone after him!"[49] From these passages it would appear that from the point of view of the Johannine Pharisees, it is Jesus who is the thief, stealing away the sheep that rightfully belong to them.

But there are two obstacles to a straightforward identification of the thief with the Jewish authorities. While there is clearly an undercurrent of rivalry in the tension between Jesus and the Jewish authorities, the principal cause of this tension, from the evangelist's perspective, is the refusal of the Pharisees as well as the majority of rank and file Jews, to believe in Jesus. In other words, what is wrong with the Jews is not so much their attempt to exert power, but their refusal to belong to his sheep. This is stated explicitly in 10:26, in which Jesus declares, "...you do not believe, because you do not belong to my sheep." Even their efforts to kill Jesus, which in 11:48 and 12:10 are associated with their efforts to stem the tide of belief in him, are understood by the evangelist as the ultimate proof of their refusal to believe in him. (cf. 7:45–52). As the Johannine Jesus says in 8:37, "you look for opportunity to kill me because there is no place in you for my word."

It is interesting to note that John 9, which is taken by many scholars as strong contextual proof for the identification of the thief as the Pharisees,[50]

---

[49] This statement is not true in a literal sense, since there are many Jews and Gentiles who do not believe in Jesus (cf. 12:38). It expresses, however, the same victory that is illustrated in the *paroimia* in 10:1–5. The flock belongs to Jesus alone: only his voice do the sheep know, and only him do they follow.

[50] For example, Quasten, 3–5.

provides the clearest demonstration that they in fact parallel those sheep who refuse to belong to Jesus. If the outstanding characteristic of Jesus' sheep is their faithful response to his voice (10:3, 4, 27), then it is the Jews' unwillingness to hear his voice or believe his words (10:25) which places them outside the fold. In contrasting the "blindness" of the Pharisees, who can physically see, with the insight of the man born blind, chapter 9 dramatizes the Jews' "deafness" as well. The Pharisees ask repeatedly for information concerning the restoration of the blind man's sight (cf. 9:15, 17, 24, 26). Finally the man himself exclaims in exasperation: "I have told you already, and you would not listen. Why do you want to hear it again?" (9:27).

Is it possible that the Jewish authorities are meant to be seen both as thieves and as "failed" sheep—i.e., as people who should have been, but refused to become, part of Jesus' flock? The difficulty in distinguishing the Jews from the Jewish authorities in many parts of the Johannine narrative[51] does not in itself pose a serious threat to the scholarly consensus. As we have already noted in our discussion of the door, the images favored by the evangelist are often distressingly fluid. More significant, however, is the association of the thief and wolf with the death of the sheep. On the surface, this would appear to support the scholarly consensus, because of the many passages which portray the Johannine Jews as trying to scatter or kill not only Jesus but also his followers. The man born blind is cast out of the synagogue (9:34). A similar fate, and worse, awaits Lazarus (12:10) and the other disciples (16:2; cf. 20:19). But if the death blow which the thief attempts to deal is to be understood as the opposite of eternal life, the physical persecution and death of the believers is irrelevant. Rather, it is the death which is the consequence of unbelief which is so threatening to the welfare of the sheep. Though the Jewish authorities are ready to kill Jesus and his followers, they do not attempt to "steal" them away from him. Where Jews are portrayed as turning away from a prior faith in Christ, the Jewish authorities are not to blame. For example, those whose departure is noted in 6:60 left Jesus because of his "hard saying", namely that "the one who eats this bread will live forever" (6:58). Similarly, according to 8:59, other Jews who had believed in him left as a reaction to his words.

Yet that there is a threat to the believers from which the shepherd—Jesus—can and must protect them is evident in the Johannine narrative. In 6:39, Jesus

---

[51] The blurred distinctions between the "Jews" and the "Jewish establishment" are evident even in those passages which provide the strongest support for the scholarly consensus. It is the Jews, not the Pharisees or other Jewish authorities who remind the man who was cured that "it is not lawful for you to carry your pallet" on the sabbath (5:10). It is the Jews who are described as persecuting Jesus (5:16) and as seeking all the more to kill him (5:18). In 9:13–18, the terms Jews and Pharisees are used interchangeably. In some passages, such as 7:25–26, however, there is a clear distinction between the Jews and their rulers.

describes as the will of the Father "that I should lose nothing of all that he has given me, but raise it up on the last day." In 17:12, this idea is reiterated in a way that emphasizes that it is the believers in Jesus who have been guarded: "While I was with them, I protected them in your name that you have given me. I guarded them, and not one of them was lost except the one destined to be lost [RSV: the son of perdition], so that the scripture might be fulfilled" (cf.18:9). This last passage not only raises the question of the identity of the one from whom the believers must be guarded, but also provides us with a clue to the answer. The "son of perdition" refers of course to Judas, who had belonged to the flock, indeed to its inner circle of disciples, but had been lost, or snatched away. In 13:2 and 27, the "thief" or "wolf" responsible for this act is clearly identified as the devil (13:2) or Satan (13:27).

Is it possible that Satan is our thief? This proposal has been made, though rather laconically, by Hugo Odeberg. Odeberg sees a parallel between the double epithets of "murderer and liar" applied to the devil in 8:44, and the reference to the "thief and bandit" in 10:1ff.[52] On this basis he suggests that the "thief" and the "bandit" should probably be identified as the διάβολος and his kin.[53] Odeberg's sole argument therefore focuses on the parallel form of the respective epithets. But this is not the only evidence in favor of this identification. More telling is the association between the devil and death in 8:44, which parallels the description of the thief and robber in 10:1–21 whose aim is to steal, kill, and destroy the sheep.

Several passages in the Fourth Gospel allude to the devil as the great adversary of Jesus in the context of the cosmological tale.[54] In 14:30, Jesus tells his disciples, "I will no longer talk much with you, for the ruler of this world is coming. He has no power over me...." In 16:11, we learn that the ruler of this world is judged.[55] This judgment is associated with the activity of the paraclete, who, in replacing Jesus in the world, also presumably takes over his role of protecting the sheep (cf. 14:25–26; 15:26; and 16:7–11, 13–14). Furthermore, it would appear that Satan continues to pose a threat to Jesus' believers even after he has "snatched" Judas, for Jesus prays to the Father that he "keep them from the evil one" (17:15).

This association implies that we will find the primary referent for our thief not in the historical tale of the gospel, but in the cosmological tale. Like the

---

[52] Odeberg, *Gospel*, 327. Many scholars, however, especially those who see the *paroimia* as an allegory, identify the wolf as the devil. For discussion, see Schnack. 2.296, and Simonis, 284.

[53] Odeberg, *Gospel*, 328.

[54] This rivalry is expressed explicitly in the Synoptic stories of the Temptation (Mark 1:12–13 and parallels).

[55] See J. C. Coetzee, "Christ," 104–21; and AB 2.706.

shepherd, the thief begins from a point outside the sheepfold, and must be distinguished from the sheep themselves. These characteristics are not true of the Pharisees and other Jewish leaders, but are true of the devil. Furthermore, the devil, or the ruler of this world, has indeed entered the world, the sheepfold, but not by the door, i.e., through incarnation and by being sent by the Father, but by some other, unspecified, way.

Finally, it may be noted that Satan's presence in the world preceded that of Jesus. As the ruler of this world (14:30; 16:11), it is from his reign that the world—shrouded in darkness (1:5)—requires salvation, for which purpose God has sent his Son (3:17). That the believers—except for Judas—have not heeded this thief is indicated by the fact that, though they are in the world (17:15, 18), "they do not belong to the world," just as Jesus does not (17:16).

It would seem, therefore, that Satan fits the description of the thief more completely than do the Jewish authorities. But we must not be too hasty in acquitting the latter of attempted robbery and murder. The language of 10:8 implies that the robber and thief is not one figure but many. At least this detail of the thief's description suits the Jewish authorities more readily than it does Satan. But the difficulty is resolved by the shepherd himself, who in 8:44 describes the Jews as the children of the devil. This close link between our two candidates is demonstrated by the similarities in their behavior: the Jews, like the devil, are murderers and liars. Offensive as these words are to our modern sensibilities, they allow us to see that for the Johannine Jesus, the Jews are the henchmen of the devil, who accomplish his work in the world. This implies that while it is Satan who coheres most closely with the figure of the thief and the wolf in the cosmological tale, it is the Jews who at least to some degree were doing his work in the first-century Palestine setting of the historical tale, just as Jesus was accomplishing the work of God (17:4).

Summary. Whereas most scholars situate the *paroimia* in the historical tale, we have attempted to place the elements of 10:1–5 and the relationships among them in the context of the cosmological tale. The parallels among *paroimia*, historical, ecclesiological, and cosmological tales are outlined in the following chart:

Paroimia	Historical	Ecclesiological	Cosmological
shepherd	Jesus	Jesus/leaders[56]	the "Word"
sheep	Jews	Joh. community	humankind
his own sheep	believers	Joh. community	believers
sheepfold	Jewish theocracy	?	world
thief/robber	Jewish leaders	Jewish leaders	Satan (8:44)
door	?	Jesus?[57]	Jesus' birth/death
gatekeeper	?	Jesus?	the Baptist

This chart illustrates two points. The first is that the cosmological tale is, in our judgment, able to account more naturally for all of the elements of the *paroimia* than are the other two tales. Because the elements in the *paroimia* are understood as corresponding to, or being parallel to, a structure outside the passage itself, namely specific characters within the cosmological tale, our reading of the passage is an allegorical one.[58] Second, and more important, while the parallels between the *paroimia* and the other two tales are, except perhaps for the sheepfold, apt as far as they go, they themselves may be placed within the universal framework of the cosmological tale.

JOHN 10:1–5 IN CONTEXT

Our reading of the *paroimia* has placed the elements of 10:1–5 and the relationships among them in the context of the cosmological tale. Not only the parallels in structure and the clues in 10:7–18 but also the immediate and extended contexts of chapter 10 support this reading of the passage. Chapter 9 is seen by most scholars as an important key to the meaning of the *paroimia*. Because there is no indication of a change in narrative context between the end of chapter 9 and the beginning of chapter 10, many scholars have posited a thematic connection between the two episodes.[59] The Pharisees exemplify the thieves and robbers, whereas the man born blind is one of the sheep who knows

---

[56] I.e., the leaders of the Johannine community.

[57] This is according to Painter's analysis.

[58] This does not mean, however, that the *paroimia* "is" an allegory; rather, it indicates only that the interpretation being offered here is allegorical to the extent that referents outside the passage are suggested for the major elements of the *paroimia*.

[59] See Quasten, 3–5; Hoskyns, *The Fourth Gospel*, 366; AB 1:377. Guilding (*Fourth Gospel*, 129) argues that this is actually a forced interpretation; the passage appears where it does because of its place in the sequence of lectionary readings.

Jesus (9:37) and follows, or believes in, him (9:38). More precisely, however, Jesus leads the man out of his state of blindness to sight, just as he leads the sheep, or the dead, from the sheepfold. The man, when blind, hears Jesus' voice commanding him: "Go, wash in the pool of Siloam" (9:7). His obedience to this command results in the restoration of his sight. Hence the man's transition from blindness to sight can be described as a passage from darkness to light, from unbelief to belief, and hence, from death to life. Furthermore, it is based on his ability to hear, and to heed, the voice of the "shepherd."

These observations suggest that the contrast between darkness and light is another way of expressing the crucial change in state from being within the sheepfold to being outside it, from condemnation to salvation and from death to life, as implied in our reading of 10:1–5. This world is like the realm of the dead, the realm of darkness, whereas emergence from death not only brings the dead back to life but also back into the world of light.[60] This is also implied in 1:4: "In him was life, and the life was the light of all people."[61]

The language of light and darkness is picked up again in the introduction to the Lazarus miracle, which, like chapter 9, is part of the narrative context of our *paroimia*. The Johannine Jesus, having decided to travel to Judea in response to the appeal by Lazarus' sisters, assures his worried disciples (11:9–10): "Are there not twelve hours of daylight? Those who walk during the day do not stumble, because they see the light of this world. But those who walk at night stumble, because the light is not in them." Jesus then proceeds to Bethany, where he calls Lazarus—who, like the man born blind, hears his voice—back to life (11:43–44).

Therefore in the gospel as a whole, the *paroimia* and the entire chapter which explicates and extends its images are framed by two episodes which portray the emergence of Jesus' followers from darkness to light, from blindness to sight in the case of the man born blind, and more dramatically, from death to life in the case of Lazarus. This emergence is the consequence of their ability to hear the voice of Jesus and to follow him. This parallels the movement of the sheep from the sheepfold to outside it, also predicated on the sheep's hearing and heeding their shepherd's voice.

---

[60] It is interesting to note that many Egyptian texts refer to the realm of the dead as a place of darkness. For examples, see J. Zandee, *Death as an Enemy According to Ancient Egyptian Conceptions* (Leiden: Brill, 1960) 88–91. The connection between death and darkness is also apparent in some biblical passages, such as Ps 107:10–16, and especially Job 10:21.

[61] Of even greater interest is 8:12, in which Jesus declares: "I am the light of the world, he who follows me will not walk in darkness, but will have the light of life." This passage, like the *paroimia* in 10:1–5, uses imagery to describe the relationship between Jesus and those who follow him, but it defines the terms of the imagery: Jesus is the light; the light is life; those who follow Jesus, therefore "have" life.

The idea that leaving the sheepfold in response to the shepherd's voice is like passing from death to life is not only implied in the structure of cosmological tale, but is also suggested by verbal parallels between the *paroimia* and two passages in the gospel which explicitly discuss resurrection. The first passage is 5:24–29, in which Jesus says to the Jews:

> Very truly, I tell you, anyone who hears my word [ὅτι ὁ τὸν λόγον μου ἀκούων] and believes him who sent me has eternal life, and does not come into judgment, but has passed from death to life. Very truly, I tell you, the hour is coming, and is now here, when the dead will hear the voice of the Son of God [ὅτε οἱ νεκροὶ ἀκούσουσιν τῆς φωνῆς τοῦ υἱοῦ τοῦ θεοῦ], and those who hear will live.... Do not be astonished at this; for the hour is coming when all who are in their graves will hear his voice and come out [ἀκούσουσιν τῆς φωνῆς αὐτοῦ καὶ ἐκπορεύσονται]—those who have done good, to the resurrection of life, and those who have done evil, to the resurrection of condemnation.

Jesus' power to enable others to pass "from death to life" as described in the above verses is illustrated, as we have already noted briefly above, in a second passage, in which Jesus raises his dead friend Lazarus in the following way: "he cried with a loud voice [ταῦτα εἰπὼν φωνῇ μεγάλῃ], 'Lazarus, come out!' The dead man came out [ἐξῆλθεν], his hands and feet bound with strips of cloth, and his face wrapped in a cloth" (11:43–44).

In both of these passages, Jesus is portrayed as having direct access, through his words or voice, to the realm of the dead. In both, the relationship between Jesus and the dead is expressed in language reminiscent of 10:3: the shepherd calls his sheep by name (φωνεῖ κατ' ὄνομα); they hear his voice (τῆς φωνῆς αὐτοῦ ἀκούει) and come forth (πορεύεται, ἐξάγει, ἐκβάλῃ) from the sheepfold. In 5:25–29, Jesus calls the dead, who hear his voice and emerge from the tombs.[62] In 11:43–44, Jesus calls the dead Lazarus *by name*; he presumably hears Jesus' voice, for he rises up out of his tomb.

The verbal parallels between these two passages and the *paroimia* in John 10 are matched by the similarity in the pattern of movement. Each passage presents an individual or group in some enclosure—the sheepfold in the case of 10:3, the tomb in 5:25–29 and 11:43–44. The hero, the shepherd Jesus, then calls the name of the ones who are in the enclosure. They hear his voice and emerge from the enclosure. These in turn bear some similarity to the structure of chapter 9, in

---

[62] For a discussion of this referent of "the dead" in this passage, see van der Watt, "John 5:25–9."

which the man emerges from the darkness that is blindness in response to hearing Jesus' words.

Although Jesus' ability to grant eternal life, as described in 5:24–29 and 11:1–44, is not explicitly related in these passages to his own physical death and resurrection by which he departs from the world, elsewhere throughout the gospel this connection is made very clear. Especially significant for our purposes is 10:11–18. In 10:10, Jesus declares that in contrast to the thief, who "comes only to steal and kill and destroy" the sheep, "I came that they may have life, and have it abundantly." This description of Jesus' mission is followed immediately by his self-identification as the good shepherd and the declaration that "the good shepherd lays down his life for the sheep" (10:11).

This idea is repeated in 10:15 ("and I lay down my life for the sheep") and again, several times, in 10:17–18:

> For this reason the Father loves me, because I lay down my life in order to take it up again. No one takes it from me, but I lay it down of my own accord. I have power to lay it down, and I have power to take it up again. I have received this commandment from my Father.

In these latter two verses, Jesus' death and resurrection are referred to several times and are interpreted not as acts of which Jesus is the passive object but as demonstrations of his divinely-given power.

The context of these references draws a clear connection between Jesus' death and resurrection—his departure from the world—and the eternal life of the believers (10:10, 12–14). It also emphasizes the necessity of Jesus' death for the gathering together of his flock (10:16; cf. 12:24). These comments drawn from the immediate context of the *paroimia* as well as from the rest of the gospel support the conclusion that the *paroimia*, while having some parallels to the historical tale, is most naturally situated in the context of the cosmological tale. One can therefore retell the *paroimia* in plain language as follows:

Truly, truly, I say to you, anyone who was not sent by the Father but entered the world a different way is the evil one, or Satan. The one who was sent by God and became flesh is the savior of humankind. It is to him that John the Baptist bore witness, and those who heard him believed in him. He called his own by name and led them out of the world, so that while still in the world, they were not of the world. When he had led them all out, he went ahead of them out of the world by means of his death and resurrection, back to the realm of the Father from which he came. His believers will follow him to the Father because they have heard, understood, and accepted his message. They will not follow anyone else, not even the evil one, but they will flee from him because they do not recognize the validity of his message or his power.

CONCLUSION

The foregoing analysis of each element of the *paroimia* indicates that, like most of the gospel, the passage can be read in the context of both the historical and the cosmological tales. Furthermore, like the other figurative elements of the gospel—in narrative and in discourse—it is the cosmological level, in the form of the cosmological tale, which provides the interpretive framework for the historical tale.

The relationships among the various elements parallel in structure the relationships among important characters in the historical tale. That is, the relationships among the shepherd, the sheep, and the thief are seen as corresponding to those between Jesus, his followers and the Jews or Jewish authorities in the historical tale. These parallels are apt in the sense that within the plot of the historical tale, the conflict which propels the actions is that between Jesus and his followers, on the one hand, and the Jews or Jewish authorities on the other hand. But these elements themselves within the historical tale parallel the relationship between Jesus, the one whom God sent, and those who follow him on the one hand, and Jesus and his opponents, such as the ruler of this world, on the other hand. Just as the shepherd's activity is described vis-à-vis the sheepfold, so is Jesus' activity described with respect to the world. Therefore if the cosmological tale provides the temporal and spatial framework for the historical tale, it does so as well for the specific *paroimia* under consideration.

Support for this conclusion may be found in 16:25–33, in which the term *paroimia* appears again. This passage comes at the conclusion of Jesus' farewell words to his disciples. In 16:25, he tells his disciples, "I have said these things to you in figures of speech [ἐν παροιμίαις]. The hour is coming when I will no longer speak to you in figures [ἐν παροιμίαις], but will tell you plainly [παρρησίᾳ] of the Father." He explains to the disciples that "the Father himself loves you, because you have loved me and have believed that I came from God [or: the Father]" (16:27). That is, they are beloved because of their understanding of, and belief in, Jesus as described in the cosmological tale. Jesus then concludes by offering a concise summary of the tale: "I came from the Father and have come into the world; again, I am leaving the world and going to the Father" (16:28).

The disciples respond by acknowledging that what he has just told them is—finally!—the plain meaning of the figurative language that he has been speaking in, not only in John 16 and in the farewell discourses, but, we would suggest, throughout the gospel as a whole: "Yes, now you are speaking plainly [ἐν παρρησίᾳ], not in any figure of speech [παροιμίαν]! Now we know that you know all things, and do not need to have anyone question you; by this we believe that you came from God" (16:29–30).

This passages confirms what we have surmised on the basis of our analysis of the literary technique of the gospel, namely that it is the cosmological tale which provides the frame of reference for the figurative language and imagery in the Fourth Gospel. The presence of 16:25–33 at the end of Jesus' speeches to his disciples implies that this is true not only of the immediate context but extends throughout the gospel as a whole. The presence of the word *paroimia* in both 10:6 and 16:25 would lead the implied reader to apply this insight to our passage as well.

5

HISTORY, COSMOLOGY, AND THE JOHANNINE COMMUNITY

The *paroimia* of the shepherd and the sheep is a prime example of the multiple and multivalent readings to which the Gospel of John lends itself. The debate in scholarly circles, to which the present study is intended to contribute, concerns the meaning which the implied reader would have assigned to this passage. In narratological terms, therefore, the terms of the *paroimia* as well as the structure of the relationships among these terms constitute a set of signifiers, and the discussion concerns the particular signified or narrative content, or referents of those signifiers.

With respect to this specific issue, we have argued that these signifiers, while they do correspond to objects in the "real world," also point to the various tales or stories signified by the narrative text as a whole. They can be read on the basis of the historical tale as a reference to the conflict between Jesus and the Jewish authorities, or in the context of the ecclesiological tale and its central conflict between the Johannine and Jewish communities in late first-century Asia Minor. We have argued, however, that just as the cosmological tale provides the larger frame of reference to the historical and ecclesiological tales in the gospel as a whole, so too does it provide the most complete and meaningful interpretation of the various elements of the *paroimia* and their interrelationships. In that sense, therefore, the cosmological tale serves as the interpretive key, narrative content, or ultimate signified for this set of signifiers.

The cosmological reading of the *paroimia* which I have offered is of course my particular reading of the text. It has been influenced by many factors external to the text, including the interpretive community comprised of New Testament scholars who have also provided readings of the text as well as the norms for exegetical work in the academy, and by my own interest in reader–oriented literary theory and its possible contributions to New Testament studies.

From this vantage point, the analysis of the *paroimia* serves not only to illustrate the role of the cosmological tale as interpretive key to the gospel narrative, but also to contribute to our understanding of the relationships among the implied author, the gospel stories, and the implied reader, all of which are constructs of the narrative text.

The implied author is the image we readers construct of the one who provides the elements of the narrative text, such as its symbols, plot, characters, and dialogue. Through these elements and their interrelationships within the narrative, we discern the intent of the implied author, which is to have an impact on his readers. Specifically, he shares with his readers his own perspective on Jesus and on the significance of Jesus for human existence and invites his readers to adopt this perspective as their own.

This perspective is conveyed by the three levels of story told by the gospel narrative and particularly by the relationships among them. The first level or primary tale is the historical tale, which describes the life and times of the "historical" Jesus, that is, the one who, according to gospel, lived at a particular time and place in human history.[1] The second level is the ecclesiological level. The presence of this tale is discerned by real readers who find anachronisms and other oddities in the gospel narrative which in their view pertain to the life and times of the Johannine community. This tale we have labelled the sub-tale. As such, it is not an explicit referent of the historical tale or of the narrative text itself. Furthermore, it is not discernible to all readers, since it requires specialized information and a particular point of view on the gospel narrative which are probably to be associated with Johannine scholars and, we might also suggest, the historical members of the Johannine community. The third level is the cosmological tale, which, we have argued, is the meta-tale. It constitutes the larger frame of reference for the temporal, spatial, and theological aspects of the other two tales and provides the interpretive key for discrete symbols and pericopes of the narrative text.

The implied reader and her or his response to the narrative text can be discerned on two levels. In the first place, the implied reader responds to the gospel as an individual. As such, he or she encounters in this gospel the story of another individual who, for all of his specific traits, shares some human characteristics with the reader. On this level, the cosmological tale operates as a commentary on the historical tale, by placing it into context and providing interpretations of its component events. At many points, these interpretations serve to modify the general expectations, cultural norms, conventions, and pre-understandings which the implied reader might bring to the text. For example, an encounter with Jesus' activities as recounted in the signs-narratives might suggest that Jesus is a miracle worker; the comments of the narrator as well as the

---

[1] This "historical" Jesus is not to be equated with THE historical Jesus, whom historical critics aim to construct or reconstruct from the historical tales told by the four gospels and whatever other material they define as having evidential value.

Johannine Jesus himself refocus the attention of the implied reader on the cosmological tale in which the signs are the expression of the relationship between Father and Son. Similarly, a first reaction to the crucifixion event might be anger and sorrow, until the reader recognizes the positive significance of that event within the cosmological tale. The cosmological tale, as meta-tale, in effect functions to re-direct the attention of the individual reader from a mundane and time-bound understanding of the gospel narrative as encounter with a historical individual to a broader and more universal interpretation of the gospel as the ever-valid tale of the Son of God. In effect, the cosmological tale therefore serves to de-historicize the gospel so that it is seen as ever applicable and relevant.

But the Gospel of John speaks not only to that private individual who comes to the text with only his or her own idiosyncrasies as well as a package of cultural norms and expectations. Like other New Testament books, the Fourth Gospel is addressed to a particular group of readers. Most scholars identify this group with the Johannine church, whose members lived at the time and in the community of the "real" author of this text and who therefore would have possessed the specific information and perspectives necessary to discern the ecclesiological tale. Although, as we have noted, the cosmological tale is phrased in terms which can include readers of any place and time, those very features which broaden the scope and application of the historical tale would have functioned to legitimate and intensify the Christian identification of the Johannine community.[2] This emerges most clearly in the concept of discipleship, as it appears in the historical tale and is modified and broadened by the cosmological tale.

A reader of the historical tale might conclude that the disciples who were direct followers of Jesus, and therefore eyewitnesses to his acts and words, had access to a special experience and knowledge which later Christians are denied. But the cosmological tale counteracts this view in several ways. In Jesus' prayer, which is the climax and conclusion of the farewell discourses, he explicitly includes those who come to faith through the activity—presumably including the preaching—of his disciples. As we have argued, this prayer, along with the emphasis on the work of the paraclete and the open-ended temporal framework of the cosmological tale, which concludes only with the coming of the *eschaton*, indicates the soteriological equality of post-Easter believers with those who were eyewitnesses of Jesus in his earthly ministry.

---

[2] For a different view of the relationship between elements of what we have termed the cosmological tale and the situation of the Johannine community, see Meeks, "Man from Heaven," Ashton, 163–65.

This equality is also indicated by the emphasis on hearing the word, which is important both in the *paroimia* in 10:1–5 and throughout the gospel narrative as a whole. It is significant that the sheep are not described as seeing the face of the shepherd and recognizing him visually, but as hearing his voice and recognizing him aurally. Hence it is through his words that people are led out of the world of darkness to the world of light.[3]

The positive relationship between hearing and belief is expressed directly in other passages as well. For example, in 5:24, Jesus tells his listeners: "Very truly, I tell you, anyone who hears my word and believes him who sent me, has eternal life...." In 8:43, Jesus rebukes the Jews: "Why do you not understand what I say? It is because you cannot accept [literally: are not able to hear] my word."

Not hearing the words is equated with not believing the words, and therefore not understanding the works of Jesus. These equations are illustrated in the story of the man born blind, as we have already noted.[4] According to 9:13, the Pharisees were not present to witness the healing of the man born blind. They were told of the event by the man born blind and by others who had observed his new-found ability but not the way in which the change had occurred (9:8–12). According to 9:18, "The Jews did not believe that he had been blind and received his sight" until his parents confirmed the information. Most important, they did not believe the blind man's testimony concerning the event itself. In 9:27, the blind man says, "I have told you already, and you would not listen. Why do you want to hear it again? Do you also want to become his disciples?"

In addition to this negative illustration of the connection, the gospel provides several positive illustrations. Indeed, a careful examination of the narratives recounting the call of the first disciples (1:35–53) as well as the conversion of the Samaritan community (4:39–42) reveals that almost all of the true believers in the gospel came to Jesus originally through the words of others. The first two disciples who follow Jesus and stay with him are prompted to do so not only by seeing Jesus, but also by hearing what John the Baptist said about him: "Here is [literally: Behold] the Lamb of God..." (1:29). Peter (1:42) came because of the words of his brother Andrew: "We have found the Messiah..." (1:41). Nathanael is persuaded by Philip, who says, "We have found him about whom Moses in the Law and also the prophets wrote..." (1:45).[5] The same pattern is present in chapter 4. The Samaritan woman believes on the basis of Jesus' words, which told her all she ever did (4:29). Other Samaritans come out

---

3 For a recent study of this theme, see Koester, "Hearing, Seeing, and Believing."

4 See pages 93–94 above.

5 The exception is Philip, who follows Jesus upon hearing the word of Jesus himself: "Follow me" (1:43).

of the city toward Jesus on the basis of the Samaritan woman's testimony. Similarly, "it was because they heard that he had performed this sign that the crowds went to meet him [Jesus]" (12:18).

Although the readers do not hear Jesus first-hand, his words are available to them, at great length, within the gospel itself. The implied author emphasizes the reliability of its witness, a witness apparently based primarily on the reports of the Beloved Disciple, by declaring, with respect to the piercing of Jesus' side, "He who saw this has testified so that you also may believe. His testimony is true, and he knows that he tells the truth so that you also may believe" (19:35). This is reiterated in 21:24, which describes the Beloved Disciple as "the disciple who is testifying to these things and has written them, and we know that his testimony is true." The Johannine Jesus himself focuses attention on the presence of all of the disciples as witnesses to virtually every act and word attributed to him, when he tells them: "you also are to testify, because you have been with me from the beginning" (15:27).[6] It is these acts and also, it would seem, Jesus' words[7] that are referred to in 20:30–31 as the basis of the readers' christological knowledge, faith, and eternal life.

That hearing the word is more important than being an eyewitness to Jesus is indicated in two additional passages. One example is found in 4:48, in which Jesus rebukes the nobleman for requiring signs and wonders as a basis for his faith. Here, as in 20:30–31, the reader is addressed directly and cautioned not to privilege knowledge based on direct experience. This is emphasized by the signs-story in 4:46–54 as a whole. The nobleman believes Jesus' word that the son will live before he sees this son for himself (4:50), just as the servants, who witnessed the cure but not the one who cured, believe on the basis of what they presumably have been told by the nobleman (4:53). This coheres with 20:29, in which Jesus' words to doubting Thomas emphasize the equality, if not the superiority, of those who believe without seeing to those who require tangible proof.

It is therefore hearing the word, and not seeing the work or the worker himself, which is crucial in the process of developing faith in Jesus, following him from darkness to light, and passing from death to life. Hearing the word can be accomplished not only by listening to Jesus himself, as eye-witnesses were able to do, or by listening to the words of his disciples, but also by reading this gospel in which the words, as transmitted by the Beloved Disciple and the other

---

6 The exception is Jesus' encounter with the Samaritan woman, in which the narrator is emphasizing Jesus' willingness to offend Jewish sensibilities by remaining alone with an "unclean" woman (4:9, 27).

7 Although only the σημεῖα are mentioned specifically in 20:30–31, many scholars interpret this usage in a wider sense to include the entire range of Jesus' activity as narrated in the gospel. See Bultmann, 698; Martyn, *History and Theology*, 93.

disciples with the utmost reliability, are recorded. Hence the emphasis on hearing the word, and the soteriological equality between Jesus' first followers and his later followers, would have contributed to the positive self-definition of the Johannine community in which this gospel had a special place. Despite its temporal and geographical distance from the earthly life of Jesus, the Johannine community whose story is encoded in the ecclesiological tale of the Fourth Gospel, could therefore claim spiritual authority and inclusion in the community of the saved, both because it possessed the paraclete and because through its gospel it too "heard" the words of Jesus.

These comments suggest that just as the cosmological tale conveys the narrator's perspective on the historical tale, so does it provide meaning for the ecclesiological tale, and therefore the soteriological experience of the Johannine community. In this way, all readers, implied or real, first-century or twentieth, are invited by the cosmological tale of the Fourth Gospel to see themselves as members of the flock of Jesus' "own," who hear the voice of the shepherd. Though not of the world, they remain in the world, protected from the evil one until their shepherd will return to lead them out of the fold to their Father's house.

APPENDIX:
THE DESCENT OF THE SHEPHERD

Throughout this study, we have noted a three-fold pattern of movement that is present in the cosmological tale as well as in the *paroimia* in 10:1–5. Within the cosmological tale, Jesus leaves his Father and descends to the world, is active in the world, and then ascends from the world to rejoin the Father. The lives of those who come to believe in him mirror this three-fold pattern: they are born into the world and must live there for a time, but through their faith in Jesus as the Christ, Son of God, they too depart to join the Father. This pattern of movement provides one of the keys to the cosmological interpretation of 10:1–5. The activity of the shepherd and the sheep parallels that of Jesus and the believers in the cosmological tale: the shepherd enters the sheepfold, gathers up his sheep, and then departs, followed by the sheep.

The language of descent and ascent to describe the movement of the shepherd vis-à-vis the world, along with the negative description of the world as a place of spiritual death, raises a rather tantalizing suspicion in the mind of this reader. Do we have in the gospel in general, and in the *paroimia* in particular, a hint concerning the descent of Jesus into the netherworld?

The belief that Christ descended to the realm of the dead is expressed explicitly in the Apostles' Creed.[1] This creed states in part: "Christ Jesus...was crucified under Pontius Pilate and buried. He descended to hell. On the third day He rose again from the dead, He ascended to heaven...."[2] While the clause referring to Christ's descent is not present in the Old Roman Creed, it is given as fact in the commentary on the Apostles' Creed by Tyrannius Rufinus, who argues that

> ...the fact that He descended to hell is unmistakably prophesied in the Psalms....[Upon his resurrection] He returned victoriously from the dead, bringing with Him spoils from hell. For He conducted forth those

---

[1] It is absent, however, from some other creeds, such as the old Roman creed. See John Leith, *Creeds of the Churches: A Reader in Christian Doctrine from the Bible to the Present* (rev. ed.; Richmond, Va: John Knox, 1973) 22–33.

[2] Ibid., 24.

whom death held prisoners, as He Himself had prophesied in the words: "When I am lifted up from the earth I will draw all things to myself."[3]

Although Rufinus' commentary belongs to the late fourth century,[4] most scholars agree that the descent motif is implied in several New Testament passages. 1 Pet 3:18–19, for example, to which Rufinus also appeals,[5] refers to "Christ...being put to death in the flesh but made alive in the spirit; in which he went and preached to the spirits in prison...." Eph 4:8 states that before his ascension, Christ "had also descended into the lower parts of the earth...." In Rev 1:18, Jesus tells the seer, "I died and behold I am alive for evermore, and I have the keys of Death and Hades."[6] Furthermore, at least one New Testament writer used pastoral language to discuss the death and resurrection of Jesus. The author of the Letter to the Hebrews addresses God as "the God of peace who brought again from the dead our Lord Jesus, the great shepherd of the sheep, by the blood of the eternal covenant..." (Heb 13:20).[7]

The belief in Jesus' ascent fills a gap in the Johannine narrative and the tales of Jesus to which that narrative points. This gap concerns Jesus' whereabouts and activity during the time between his death and his resurrection/ascension to the Father. An intriguing feature of the descent motif is that the pattern of movement that it implies parallels that of the cosmological tale and the shepherd *paroimia:* Jesus' descent into and ascent from the netherworld mirrors Jesus' descent into and ascent from the world in the cosmological tale and the shepherd's entrance into and departure from the sheepfold in 10:1–5. Furthermore, Jesus' ascent from the world and the shepherd's departure from the sheepfold, followed by the believers/sheep, is directly related in the gospel to resurrection, which may also be seen as a departure from the netherworld or the realm of the dead.

---

[3] Tyrannius Rufinus, *A Commentary on the Apostles' Creed* (trans. J.N.D. Kelly; New York: Newman, 1954) 61–62.

[4] See Ibid., 3–14, for an introductory discussion about the author and the dating of this work.

[5] Ibid., 61.

[6] Other allusions are often found in Heb 13:20; Rom 10:7; 14:9; Phil 2:10. For a discussion of the New Testament evidence, see Josef Kroll, *Gott und Hölle: Der Mythos vom Descensuskampfe* (Leipzig: B. G. Teubner, 1932) 1–12; J. A. MacCulloch (*The Harrowing of Hell: A Comparative Study of an Early Christian Doctrine* [Edinburgh: T. and T. Clark, 1930] 65–66) sees allusions to this motif in John 5:21, 29; 6:40; 8:56 and 11:25, but does not mention 10:1–5 in this context. J. B. Russell (*Satan: The Early Christian Tradition* [Ithaca and London: Cornell University Press, 1981] 118 and n. 34) says that hints of the descent motif appear in the New Testament, but its meaning is left undefined. The first to refer to it explicitly was Hippolytus in his work on the Antichrist; by the second century it was already very popular.

[7] Cf. also Revelation 20–21.

The motif of Jesus' descent into the netherworld is not made explicit in the Fourth Gospel. John 5:24–29 and 11:43–44, however, do describe Jesus' rescuing the dead from their tombs. Although in these passages Jesus does not descend bodily, it might be said that he descends vocally: it is by hearing Jesus' voice that the dead, exemplified by Lazarus, depart from the tomb and experience resurrection. Since, as we have already noted,[8] these passages share some of the features of 10:1–5, including vocabulary and structure (entry/exit/salvation), it seems reasonable to ask whether the implied reader might have read the *paroimia* as a reference not only to the Word's descent into and ascent from the world, but also to the Word's descent into and ascent from the netherworld.

In order to investigate this possibility, we must move beyond the intrinsic data supplied by the gospel narrative. First, it will be necessary to examine whether the extrinsic data which the implied readers, or intended audience, brought to their reading of the text would have led them to find allusion to Jesus' descent into the netherworld in John 10:1–5. Second, it will be necessary to look at whether there is any evidence that the *paroimia* was read as a reference to Jesus' descent by later readers. To address these questions will also allow us to explore the intersection between a reader-oriented approach and two more traditional approaches to the Fourth Gospel, namely *Religionsgeschichte* and the history of interpretation.

HISTORY OF RELIGIONS BACKGROUND

Biblical Allusions. Shepherds, sheep, sheepfolds, as well as the dangers posed by thieves, wolves and careless hirelings, were no doubt part of everyday experience in the Greco-Roman world. As we have seen in chapter three, some scholars view this experience as the source of the pastoral terminology and structure of the *paroimia*. This seems unlikely, however, in view of the fact that the specific details of the *paroimia*, especially the structure or sequence of its actions, correspond closely to the structure of the cosmological tale of the gospel narrative and have features in common with the historical tale as well. Nevertheless, since sheep spend the night in folds, shepherds take them out to pasture, and thieves threaten the integrity and welfare of the flock, it would appear that at least in a general way the implied author expected his readers to draw not only on their reading of the gospel but also on their own experience in order to come to some understanding of the *paroimia*.

Shepherds, sheep, and related pastoral figures populated not only the hillsides of the Greco-Roman world, but also the pages of Greco-Roman,

---

[8] See page 95 above.

biblical, and post-biblical literature. The "shepherd," "flock," and other pastoral images appear frequently in the Hebrew Bible and post–biblical Jewish and Christian literature.[9] Both Moses (Exodus 3) and David (1 Sam 17:15) are said to have been actual shepherds, caring for real sheep prior to their becoming leaders of the Israelites. Indeed, the Hellenistic Jewish exegete and philosopher Philo saw shepherding as a necessary prerequisite for political power and kingship.[10] In the Psalms and prophetic writings, the shepherd and related pastoral images are used to express the relationship of the rulers to the ruled, namely the people Israel (cf. Ezekiel 34; Zechariah 11).[11] The figurative use of shepherd as ruler is present also in 1 Enoch 89–90 and in the New Testament (e.g., Heb 13:20). Some of these passages depict a positive relationship between the shepherd and the sheep (e.g., Psalm 23, where the shepherd is God); others, a critique of shepherds who have not cared properly for those under their care (e.g., Zechariah 11). The figurative use of shepherd to mean king is found also in ancient Near Eastern and Egyptian sources. In the latter, this usage is applied not only to living rulers, but to the image of the ruler of the world to come, as well as to the god of the underworld.[12]

The paroimia makes no explicit reference to the kingship motif, though the relationship between shepherd and sheep, in which the shepherd assumes leadership over, and responsibility for, the sheep, is certainly hierarchical.[13] Although scholarly discussions of the biblical and post-biblical background of John 10 vary in length, detail, and emphasis, one may discern certain general trends.[14] While some recognize the royal connotation of the biblical image of the shepherd, few see this as operative in the paroimia or accompanying discourse. According to Bultmann, for example, there are no traces of the royal figure in

9 S.v. πρόβατον, TDNT 6.689–692; s.v. ποιμήν, TDNT 6.485–502.
10 See Philo, Jos. 2–4; Vit. Mos. 1.60–64. Unless otherwise indicated, quotations of Philo and classical literature are from the Loeb editions.
11 Bultmann (364–65) notes that this connection is common to oriental and Greek antiquity; in the Hebrew Bible, however, it is not normally developed at length but reduced to allusions and metaphors.
12 S.v. ποιμήν, TDNT 6.486.
13 In 1 Enoch, however, there is a distinction made between the Lord of the sheep (89:16, 28) and those leaders whom the Lord has raised up from among the flock, as in 89:45 "And the Lord of the sheep sent the sheep (Samuel) to another sheep (David) and raised it to become a ram and to lead the sheep instead of that ram which had abandoned its lead." Here it is clear that the king David and the prophet Samuel were leaders from within the people, while the Lord of the sheep is a leader from outside, so to speak. See The Book of Enoch or 1 Enoch: A New English Edition (ed. Matthew Black; Leiden: Brill, 1985) 77.
14 While most commentators give a brief discussion of background, others go into this background in detail and use it as the cornerstone of their analysis. See Simonis, passim, and J. Duncan M. Derrett, "The Good Shepherd: St. John's Use of Jewish Halakah and Haggadah," ST 27 (1973) 25–50; W. Jost, ποιμήν: Das Bild vom Hirten in der biblischen Ueberlieferung und seine christologische Bedeutung (Giessen, 1939).

the *paroimia*.[15] Most scholars perceive a Davidic background to this motif, but emphasize the messianic, eschatological connotations, downplaying or ignoring the element of kingship altogether.[16]

The passages cited most frequently in discussion of the biblical background of the *paroimia* are Ezekiel 34 and Zechariah 11. In the former, the prophet speaks against the "shepherds of Israel" who have been feeding and caring only for themselves instead of the sheep (34:2–4). As a result, the sheep have been scattered (34:5) and become prey to wild beasts (34:8). The shepherds are therefore removed from their posts (34:10) and the Lord himself will seek out the sheep, gather them, and tend them (34:11–16). Zechariah 11 contains a similar critique of the shepherds' poor care of their sheep (11:15–16).

Scholars see the bad shepherds as parallel to the thieves, robbers, and hirelings of 10:1–18, whose activities are detrimental to the welfare of the sheep.[17] Hence these passages are used in support of their interpretation of the *paroimia* within the context of the historical tale. In the words of J. A. T. Robinson,

> The true people of God hear his voice, because they recognize in it the authentic note of the shepherd of God's flock; by implication the Jewish leaders, who were meant to be the shepherds of Israel (Ezek 34, Zech 11) are condemned as ἀλλότριοι, foreigners to God's people (cf. Matt 17:25f., Heb 11:34).[18]

To these prophetic passages, some scholars add *1 Enoch* 88–90, in which history, from the flood to the *eschaton*, is summarized using this kind of pastoral language. Simonis sees in *1 Enoch* 89:41–50 a reference to the sheepfold as the temple, which he argues has been taken over in John 10:1–18. Furthermore, he argues that it is the combination of themes in these chapters of *Enoch* which at least in part account for the juxtaposition of chapter 9, in which the theme is blindness and sight, with chapter 10, with its pastoral references. He too, therefore, leaves aside the royal motif in his analysis of the history-of-religions background to the passages.[19]

---

[15] This is because Bultmann (367) sees its origins in the Gnostic figure of the Revealer or Redeemer.

[16] AB 1.392; s.v. ποιμήν, TDNT 6.496. In the latter it is argued (6:488) that even in the Old Testament, the title is not used for a ruling king. Augustin George ("La Porte des Brebis," 18) sees this motif present in the OT usage of the term but does not develop it with respect to John 10. One exception is Odeberg (*Gospel*, 319), who refers to this briefly.

[17] See Simonis, 164.

[18] Robinson, "Parable," 235.

[19] Simonis, 161–65.

One notable exception to the general trend on the issue of background is found in the work of Wayne Meeks.[20] Meeks does not focus on the figure of David as the shepherd and prototype of the messianic king, but rather on Moses as he is portrayed in biblical and post-biblical literature.[21] He looks at the places where "king" and "prophet" as well as other motifs overlap and concludes that there is a "package" or confluence of motifs that are used to discuss or connote kingship. Against Bultmann, Meeks argues that "the Moses traditions provide analogies to some essential features of the 'Good Shepherd' discourse in John which were absent from the Mandaean traditions...."[22] He points to the many biblical and post-biblical references to Moses as "the shepherd of Israel" or "the faithful shepherd," a metaphor which "is connected with characteristics which have several points of similarity with the Johannine discourse." For example, the notion of judgment implicit in "hearing the voice" may be related to the theophany at Mount Sinai and the emphasis on hearing God's voice via Moses' words.[23] Further, "Moses' designation as Israel's shepherd is frequently associated with his function as intercessor or advocate,"[24] which is also operative in chapter 10. Also significant is Psalm 151 in the Dead Sea Psalms Scroll, 11QPsa, in which a parallel is drawn between David's activity as the shepherd of his flock and his later role as "leader to [God's] people and ruler over the sons of his covenant."[25]

Whether or not John 10 is seen as part of the Moses typology in this gospel,[26] the close connection in the extra-Johannine literature between the notions of shepherd and king compels us to consider whether and to what degree the element of kingship is operative in Johannine christology as expressed in this *paroimia*. Further impetus to considering this connection may be found in the fact that the verb ποιμαίνω (to tend as shepherd) is used to mean rule or govern in Rev 2:27, 12:5, and 19:15. Especially striking is Rev 7:17, which states that "the Lamb at the center of the throne will be their shepherd," providing a direct connection between kingship and the shepherd image.

Is the implied reader of the Fourth Gospel led to associate the "shepherd" image of 10:1–5 with kingship? The title "king" is applied to Jesus in several passages in the gospel, though there is some ambivalence on the part of both

---

[20] Meeks, *Prophet-King*.

[21] Cf. also Odeberg, *Gospel*, 316–17.

[22] Meeks, *Prophet-King*, 213.

[23] Ibid., 311.

[24] Ibid., 312.

[25] J. A. Sanders, *The Dead Sea Psalms Scroll* (Ithaca: Cornell University Press, 1967) 97.

[26] Some scholars do see chapter 10 in the context of the Moses typology and traditions in the Gospel. In addition to Meeks, *Prophet-King*, see T. F. Glasson, *Moses in the Fourth Gospel* (London: SCM, 1963) 81, 85, 96.

Jesus and the narrator with regard to its applicability. In 1:49, Nathanael confesses Jesus to be Son of God and King of Israel. Jesus does not deny this, but promises greater revelations than those Nathanael has already experienced (1:50–51). Since Nathanael is a "true Israelite"[27] we have in his confession an example of an Israelite recognizing Jesus as his king. A similar impression is conveyed in 12:13–15, in which a great crowd in Jerusalem at the feast of the Passover greets Jesus with the words, "Hosanna! Blessed is the one who comes in the name of the Lord—the King of Israel!" Jesus' apparent acceptance of this title is indicated by his action of riding on a young donkey, in fulfilment of the prophecy in Zech 9:9: "Look, your king is coming, sitting on a donkey's colt!" John 6:15 and 18:33–37 provide some clues as to the nature of Jesus' kingship. Jesus rejects the attempts of the Jews to make him king (6:15), presumably because of their ignorance as to the true nature of his kingship. As he explains to Pilate, "My kingdom is not from this world; if my kingdom were from this world, my followers would fight to keep me from being handed over to the Jews" (18:36). Despite his disclaimer, however, Jesus is nevertheless portrayed in this gospel as the true ruler over this world, in a cosmic sense. As such, he speaks against the present ruler of this world (14:30; 16:11) and casts him out (12:31; cf. 16:33). This implies that though he has no earthly army, Jesus is the ultimate victor in a struggle with the ruler of this world.

The identification of Jesus as King of Israel is twisted into irony in chapter 19, in which Jesus is mocked, scourged and crucified as "King of the Jews." Though Jesus may be king of Israel, that is, recognized as leader by "true Israelites," he is certainly not recognized as king of the Jews, who claim to "have no king but the emperor [RSV: Caesar]" (19:15).[28]

There are several similarities between the kingship motif in the gospel and our *paroimia* in its broader setting within chapter 10. First, the gospel alludes to a struggle between Jesus, who is "king not of this world," and the ruler of this world, in which Jesus is victorious. This may be similar to the contrast between the shepherd and the thieves, in which the shepherd is successful in gaining entry into the sheepfold and leading the sheep out. Second, just as the shepherd is followed by the sheep, the king is followed by "true" Israelites, of whom Nathanael is the prime example. Finally, there are many who do not recognize or follow the King of Israel, recognizing neither his leadership nor his kingship. That there are some sheep who are not the shepherd's own is hinted at by the

---

[27] Brown (AB 1.83) translates the Greek as "a genuine Israelite," whereas Bultmann (104, note 4) prefers a more descriptive translation, "one worthy of the name of Israel."

[28] This too is an ironic statement, since one would assume that the "Jews" should have no king but God.

use of τὰ ἴδια in the *paroimia*.[29] This is made more explicit in 10:26, in which Jesus tells the Jews, "You do not believe, because you do not belong to my sheep."

Therefore there seem to be some parallels between the kingship motif as it is hinted at in the Gospel and the shepherd image as it is developed in chapter 10. This suggests that the shepherd image may have connoted not only the Messiah but also the king who rules over this world, although his authority is derived from outside it.

Classical Background: The Descent Motif. If the image of the "shepherd" leads us to the theme of kingship, the pinnacle of power, there is another figure who leads us in the opposite direction. This is the elusive gatekeeper, relegated to a secondary position in almost all interpretations of the *paroimia*. Most often he is seen simply as an incidental detail to lend verisimilitude to the pastoral setting. If he is given an identity at all, it is one which derives from his function as the guard of the sheepfold or, as in our interpretation, as John the Baptist, the one who introduces the shepherd to the sheep within the fold.

Though the gatekeeper may be difficult to place within the context of the Johannine narrative, the function which he performs is familiar to readers of ancient mythology as the gatekeeper to the netherworld. This figure usually appears in the context of a descent-myth, in which a hero, heroine, god or goddess figure descends to the realm of the dead and gains entry through a gate by means of an encounter with the gatekeeper. A Mesopotamian story describes the efforts of the goddess Innana to gain entry to the seven gates of the netherworld which are guarded by Neti.[30] She eventually succeeds and later ascends from this realm, bringing some of the dead along with her. A similar story is told of Ishtar.[31] In Egyptian sources the dead are said to pass through the series of gates guarded by demons before gaining repose.[32] The motif is not limited to the polytheistic religions but is present even in the Hebrew Bible. Psalm 24:7–10 was understood in the early centuries of the Common Era to refer to the guardians of the gates of Sheol and may itself be a fragment of a mythological story depicting the descent motif.[33] The presence of this motif in the literatures which belong to the religious and cultural background of the evangelist and his intended audience raises the possibility that in John 10 the

---

[29] Cf. Quasten, 6–7.

[30] J. B. Pritchard, ed., *Ancient Near Eastern Texts* (Princeton: Princeton University Press, 1955) 52–57.

[31] Ibid., 106–9.

[32] Zandee, *Death as an Enemy*, 114–17.

[33] See Alan Cooper, "Ps 24:7–10: Mythology and Exegesis," *JBL* 102 (1983) 37–60.

gatekeeper figure is also at some level an allusion to the gatekeeper of the underworld.

Though the gatekeeper figure in the texts we have referred to above does not appear specifically in pastoral contexts, there are some stories in which he does. One of the twelve labors of Heracles was to fetch the cattle of Geryon from Erythia, an island near the ocean. This Geryon had the body of three men grown together and joined in one at the waist, but parted in three from the flanks and thighs. He owned red cattle, herded by Eurytion and watched over by Orthus, a two-headed hound. Heracles journeyed there, killed the dog and also the herdsman. Another herdsman, called Menoites, who was there pasturing the kine of Hades, reported to Geryon what had occurred. He approached Heracles beside the river Anthemus, as he was driving away the kine, joined battle with him and was shot dead. After this, Heracles, overcoming many attempts to rob him of the cattle, embarked with the kine in a goblet, sailed across to Tartessus, and gave the goblet back to the sun (Apollodorus, *Bibl.* 2.5.10).

At first glance, this story appears to be a pastoral tale. There are indications, however, that it was seen as a descent story in the ancient world. Especially important are the references to the kine of Hades and to the watchdog, who is similar to Cerberus, known to us from *Aeneid* 6.417–19 as the watchdog to the underworld. Furthermore, Geryon is referred to in *Aeneid* 6.289 as one of inhabitants of Hades.[34] Finally, we have the curious occurrence of Menoites, the herdsman of Hades. J. H. Croon analyses the story in this way:

> He [Menoites] recurs...in Apollodorus' story of Heracles' descent into Hades. It would seem that Apollodorus (or his sources) simply gave this herdsman a role in the Geryon-story because of the close connection between the two sagas: in the one Heracles wrestles with the man who looks after the kine of the Underworld, and slaughters one of the cows; in the other he has a contest with Geryon in the "redland" for the "red cattle": it is not difficult to see, and indeed, it has often enough been observed that this "redland in the West," the land of sunset, is the Underworld itself. So Menoites and Eurytion are virtually the same person. But we can go further. Eurytion himself is superfluous in the story. His dog Orthus is a mere double of Cerberus: Geryon, the "roaring" ($\gamma\eta\rho\acute{\nu}\omega$) is the god or at any rate a daemon of the Underworld; his kine are identical with the herd of Hades. Indeed, we find him sometimes represented as pasturing the cattle himself. This may well be the original form. Of course, when later he was thought of

---

[34] H. E. Butler, *The Sixth Book of the Aeneid* (Oxford: Basil Blackwell, 1920).

as a king and ruler over the "redland," he had to delegate the mean task of the herdsman to a servant. In this way we reach the original character of one of Heracles' opponents, which we can describe as a "herdsman of the dead."[35]

If Croon's analysis is correct, this story expresses in figurative language the descent of the hero Heracles to the netherworld to take out the cattle of Geryon and return them to their rightful owner.

Similar in some ways is the twelfth labor of Heracles, recounted by Apollodorus in *Bibl.* 2.5.12.[36] This labor was to bring Cerberus—"the hound three-headed, warder of Hell-gate"[37]—from Hades. In the process, Heracles had many adventures and accomplished many tasks. Among them was the raising of Theseus from the dead and the slaughtering of one of the cattle of Hades to provide the souls of the dead with blood.[38] In doing so, he had to overcome Menoites, who tended the kine. When Heracles asked Hades, King of the netherworld, for Cerberus, Hades ordered him to take the animal provided he mastered him without the use of his weapons. Hercules found Cerberus at the gates of Acheron, managed to master him, carried him off, and ascended through Troezen.

Seneca describes this same event in *Hercules furens*, in language which has some points of contact with our *paroimia*. As the Chorus declaims:

Eurystheus, brought to the light by birth untimely, had bidden thee explore the world's foundations; this only was lacking to thy tale of labours, to despoil the king of the third estate [i.e., Hades]. Thou wast bold to enter the blind approach, where a way leads to the far-off shades, a gloomy way and fearsome with dark woods, but crowded with vast accompanying throngs....Thebes' joyful day is here. Lay hold on the altars, ye suppliants; slay the fat victims; let husbands and wives together start up the festal dance; let the tillers of the fertile field [i.e. the cattle] lay by the yoke and rest. Peace reigns by the hand of Hercules from the land of the dawn to the evening star, and where the sun, holding mid-heaven, gives to shapes no shadows....He has crossed the streams of Tartarus, subdued the gods of the underworld, and has

---

35 Johan Harm Croon, *The Herdsman of the Dead: Studies on some cults, myths and legends of the ancient Greek colonization-area* (Utrecht: Drukkerij S. Budde, 1952) 31–32.

36 For other places in classical Greek literature where this story appears, see *Apollodorus I* (LCL; Cambridge: Harvard University Press, 1921) 232, note 1.

37 Euripedes, *Hercules* (ed. Kevin Hargreaves Lee; Leipzig: B. G. Teubner, 1988) line 1276.

38 This seems to be a favorite beverage of the souls of the dead. See also Homer, *Od.* 11.30–50.

returned. And now no fear remains; naught lies beyond the underworld
(ll. 830–92).

This passage refers to the descent of Heracles/Hercules into the netherworld,
from whence he ascended after vanquishing the king of the netherworld. This
victory served to liberate the "cattle of the fields" and ensure universal peace.
The passage, like the Fourth Gospel, uses the language of light and darkness to
contrast the world of the living with the realm of the dead.

In this lengthy and complicated story, as in the story of Geryon, there are
some points of contact with our *paroimia*, especially the references to animals,
though not sheep, and to a gatekeeper who happens to be different from the king
of the netherworld. Heracles, like Jesus, has the ability to raise souls from the
dead.[39]

This last characteristic of the Greek hero is the focal point of Euripides'
Alcestis. In this play, Alcestis voluntarily dies for her husband Admetus when his
parents would not. Happening upon this distressed household, Admetus' friend
Hercules decides:

> I must save this woman who has died so lately, bring Alcestis back to
> live in this house....I must go there and watch for Death of the black
> robes, master of dead men, and I think I shall find him drinking the
> blood of slaughtered beasts beside the grave. Then, if I can break
> suddenly from my hiding place, catch him, and hold him in the circle
> of these arms, there is no way he will be able to break my hold on his
> bruised ribs, until he gives the woman up to me. But if I miss my quarry,
> if he does not come to the clotted offering, I must go down, I must ask
> the Maiden and the Master in the sunless homes of those below, and I
> have confidence I shall bring Alcestis back... (ll. 840–54).[40]

After fighting with a deity at her tomb, Heracles returns with a veiled woman
who is Alcestis, to the astonishment and joy of her husband, who cries, "...How
did you bring her back from down there to the light?" (l. 1139).

---

[39] For general discussion of Heracles and his ability to descend to the netherworld, see Josef
Fink "Heracles Held und Heiland," *Antike und Abendland* 9 (1960) 73–79; Carl Schneider,
"Herakles der Todüberwinder," *Wissenschaftliche Zeitschrift der Karl-Marx Universität* 7 (1958)
661–66. Some comparisons between Heracles and Jesus have been made in the literature. See,
for example, Friedrich Pfister, "Herakles und Christus," *ARW* 34 (1937) 42–60; Carl
Schneider, *Geistesgeschichte des Antiken Christentums* (Munich: C.H. Beck'sche
Verlagsbuchhandlung, 1954) 1.142.
[40] *The Complete Greek Tragedies* (ed. D. Grene and R. Lattimore; 4 vols.; Chicago,
University of Chicago Press, 1955) 3.40–41.

The contrast between the light of life and the darkness of death is also expressed in Theseus' description of his descent into Hades, as presented in Seneca's *Hercules furens*:

> Here the home of hateful Pluto unbars its mouth....Not in utter darkness does the way first begin; a slender gleam of the light left behind and a doubtful glow as of the sun in eclipse falls there and cheats the vision. Such light the day mingled with night is wont to give, at early dawn or at late twilight. From here ample spaces spread out, void regions, whereto the entire human race turns and hastens. It is not toil to go; the road itself draws them down... (ll. 664–75).

The chorus expresses compassion for the dead:

> O ye dead, what thoughts are yours when, light now banished, each has sorrowing felt his head o'erwhelmed 'neath all the earth? There are thick chaos, loathsome murk, night's baleful hue, the lethargy of a silent world and empty clouds (ll. 858–63).

Upon his arrival in the world, Theseus' vision is dimmed; he can hardly bear the unaccustomed light (ll. 650–53).

The expectation, or hope, of a second return of Hercules is expressed by his mother. In Seneca's tragedy *Hercules oetatus*, she proclaims:

> Once to the farthest realms of Tartarus, O son, didst thou go but to return—Oh, when from infernal Styx wilt thou come again? Not in such wise as to bring e'en spoil with thee, nor that Theseus again may owe thee the light of day,—but when, though all alone? Will the whole world, heaped on thee, hold thy shade, or the hell-hound [Cerberus] avail to keep thee back? When wilt thou batter down the Taenarian gates, or to what yawning jaws shall thy mother betake herself, where is the approach to death? Thou takes thy journey to the dead, and 'twill be thy only one (ll. 1765–75).

In *Hercules furens*, his widow begs:

> Come forth, my husband, burst through the darkness shivered by thy hand; if there is no backward way, and the road is closed, rend earth asunder and return; and whatever lies hid in the hold of murky night, let forth with thee (ll. 279–82).

Therefore these stories imply a world view in which Hades or the netherworld is ruled over by a king, perhaps Pluto, whom the hero conquers. The gates of Hades are guarded by some agent of the king, such as Cerberus, who must be taken by surprise or strength. The hero who does so can succeed in taking out a particular dead person and come out unharmed himself. This view is also expressed in Virgil's *Aeneid*, Book 6, which describes Hades as the land of sleep and shades, of drowsy night, contrasted with the land of the living, in which it is light and day.[41] Despite the stark contrasts between the two realms, communication between them is possible. Virgil provides further details concerning the architectural specifications of Hades. Its battlements are forged in the furnaces of the Cyclops (*Aeneid* 6.630)[42] and it has gates (Euripedes, *Hercules*, l. 944).

Noteworthy are the passages which describe the one who guides the souls into hell as a shepherd. In his *Olympian Odes* 9, strophe 2, Pindar describes the labor of Heracles:

How was it else the hands of Heracles could wield his club against the Trident's power, when by the walls of Pylos stood Poseidon and pressed him hard; and with his silver bow Phoebus Apollo menaced him close in battle; and Hades too spared not to ply him with that sceptred staff, which takes our mortal bodies down along the buried road to the dead world.[43]

In this passage, Hades is described as a shepherd, who with his staff leads the dead like sheep. A similar motif is also present in Homer's *Odyssey*, Book 24, which describes the descent of the suitors of Odysseus' wife Penelope to the netherworld. They were guided by Hermes,

armed with the splendid golden wand that he can use at will to cast a spell on our eyes or wake us from the soundest sleep. He roused them up and marshalled them with this....With such shrill discord the

---

[41] This contrast is implicit or explicit in many passages dealing with Hades, as is the contrast between sound and silence. Cf. George Thaniel, "Themes of Death in Roman Religion and Poetry" (Ph.D., McMaster University, 1971) 117–18.

[42] See Thaniel ("Death," 116–55) for a detailed discussion of the topography of Hades according to Virgil and others, as well as W. F. Jackson Knight, *Vergil: Epic and Anthropology* (ed. John D. Christie; New York: Barnes and Noble, 1967) 143.

[43] Pindar, *The Odes of Pindar* (trans. Geoffrey S. Conway; London: J. M. Dent, 1972) 54.

company set out in Hermes' charge, following the Deliverer down the
dark paths of decay (*Od*. 24.1–10).[44]

Our final example from classical Greek literature is the story of Odysseus'
conquest of the Cyclops, in Homer's *Odyssey*, Book 9. In this story, Odysseus and
his men sail, in total darkness, to the land of the Cyclops. There they see a large
cave and indications that large flocks of sheep and goats were generally penned
within it for the night. The cave-mouth was surrounded by a strong-walled yard.
This cave was the lair of a monstrous creature who pastured his flocks from the
cave. Odysseus, armed with potent wine, stole into the cave with twelve men,
and waited until the Cyclops returned, brought his sheep into the cave, and
rolled a giant stone over the mouth. He was enraged to see the men, and ate
about half of them, leaving Odysseus with the dilemma of how to leave the cave
alive. In the morning, the Cyclops left the cave to pasture his sheep, locking
Odysseus and the rest of his men within. Upon his return in the evening, he
again brought all the sheep in and closed up the cave. After some discussion, in
the course of which Odysseus tricked him into thinking his name is "Noman,"
Odysseus blinds the Cyclops. Since the stone had already been removed from the
mouth of the cave in order to pasture the flock, the Cyclops was forced to set
himself there, with his fingers extended across it, to catch anyone who tried to
steal through with the sheep. Odysseus and his men managed to leave the cave
by hiding under the exiting rams and sheep. They drove the flock down to the
ship "where the sight of us gladdened the others at thought of the death we had
escaped" (*Od*. 9.455; trans. E. Rieu).

Though there is no explicit reference to the descent motif in this story,
there are nevertheless some indications that this is in fact the intent, particularly
in the strong association between the cave and death.[45] This is strengthened by
the reference to the Cyclops, who, as we saw, is considered to be the blacksmith
who fashioned the walls of Hades, according to Virgil.[46] Of special interest is the
depiction of the cave—the place of death?—as a sheepfold, from which sheep
and human beings must depart in order to survive.

To summarize, these examples suggest that the descent or καΤάβασις was a

44 The translation is that of E. Rieu (*The Odyssey* [Harmondsworth, U.K.: Penguin, 1946]
351). Croon (*Herdsman*, 68) notes that Hermes is often portrayed as a herdsman in classical
Greek art.
45 Knight, *Vergil*, 144.
46 Thaniel, "Death," 89.

well-known and common motif in this literature.[47] This motif refers to a hero who descends to the netherworld, gains entry past the gatekeeper, and does battle with the King of the netherworld. Some of these stories use pastoral language; for example, they describe the one who guides the souls to Hades bearing a staff or rod, or refer to those beings who are themselves freed from a Hades-like enclosure as cattle or sheep. Some stories refer to the desire of the souls of the dead to drink the blood of slaughtered sheep or cattle. Heracles and Odysseus in particular are themselves described as shepherds or cattlemen, at least inasmuch as they take the sheep or cattle out of the deadly enclosure in which they are found.[48] Finally, in all of these stories, there is freedom of communication between the living and the dead and sometimes passage from the nether to the upper worlds.

Though it cannot be said with certainty that the implied reader's knowledge of the descent motif was assumed by the implied author of the Fourth Gospel, the popularity of these stories is hard to dispute.[49] What is interesting about them for our purposes is that they contain in a narrative context certain features which are also present in John 10:1–5. These are: the use of pastoral allusions in the depiction of the inhabitants of the netherworld and those who led them in or lead them out, the reference to a gatekeeper, as well as to a ruler of the netherworld, and the plot structure, which, as in our *paroimia* as well as in the cosmological tale of the Fourth Gospel, involves a hero who enters a physical realm, engages in some activity, and then departs, taking with him some of its inhabitants. Also of interest is the presence of the language of light and darkness, which distinguish this world from the netherworld, since a similar contrast is strongly tied to the context of our passage (cf. John 9 and 11). Given these similarities of the descent stories to John 10:1–5, it is possible that Greek-speaking readers, on encountering the *paroimia*, may have supplied associations with this complex of images and patterns that would have called to mind these descent stories and the descent motif in general.

---

[47] L. R. Farnell, *Greek Hero Cults and Ideas of Immortality* (Oxford: Clarendon, 1921) 105. For general discussion of the κατάβασις motif in classical and other ancient literatures, s.v. "Höllenfahrt," *RGG* (3rd ed.) 3.407–8; Kroll, *Gott und Hölle*; MacCulloch, *Harrowing of Hell*.

[48] These points are consistent with Farnell's observation that it is normal and usual for a hero or saint to be transformed into an agriculturalist or a shepherd in classical Greek literature. See Farnell, *Hero Cults*, 152.

[49] It is likely that Gentile readers would have been familiar with the myths and literary sources for the descent motif. Cf. Werner Jaeger, *Early Christianity and Greek Paideia* (London: Oxford University, 1961), and H. I. Marrou, *A History of Education in Antiquity* (London: Sheed and Ward, 1956) especially 160–75.

THE DESCENT MOTIF IN EARLY CHRISTIAN LITERATURE

As we have already noted, there are some allusions to the descent motif in the New Testament. For more detailed and explicit Christian expositions of the descent motif, however, we must go beyond the New Testament literature to the New Testament Apocrypha and the writings of the Church Fathers. In doing so we will also consider the question of whether any of these descent passages allude to the John 10:1–5. Because these texts all postdate the Fourth Gospel, in some cases by several centuries, they cannot in any way be regarded as sources for our *paroimia*. Nevertheless, we shall see that when these texts speak of Jesus' descent, they do so using language and imagery that is familiar to us from the Gospel of John in general and our *paroimia* in particular.

There are several passages in the apocryphal and patristic literature in which the descent motif is combined with pastoral language. For example, Irenaeus (second century C.E.) describes the purpose of Christ's descent as seeking the sheep which had perished, with whom he would ascend to the height above and enter the "many mansions in the Father's house" (John 14:2).[50] In the Easter Homily ascribed to Epiphanius, the author says that Christ—the "good shepherd"—went to Hades to seek out Adam as a lost sheep, adding, "My heavenly Father expects the sheep that was lost." Ninety-nine sheep of the angels waited for Adam, their fellow-servant, when he rose and went up and returned to God.[51] In his *Catechetical Lectures*, St. Cyril of Jerusalem (fourth century C.E.) mentions Jonah's sojourn in the whale as a type of the Descent.

> Concerning His Resurrection Isaia [sic] says: "He who brought from the earth the great shepherd of the sheep" (Isa 63:11). He has added the word "great," lest He be esteemed merely equal in honor with the shepherds before Him (*Cat.* 14.20).[52]

Finally we refer to the *Acts of Thomas*, in which Judas Thomas says to Jesus:

---

50 Irenaeus, *Adv. haer.* 3.19.3; ANCL 5.346. Unless otherwise indicated, quotations of patristic literature are from the Ante-Nicene Fathers (ANF), the Ante-Nicene Christian Library (ANCL), or the Nicene and Post-Nicene Fathers, second series (NPNF).

51 See PG 43.481, and MacCulloch (*Harrowing*, 196), who argues that the works of Pseudo-Epiphanius reveal direct knowledge of the Gospel of Nicodemus and other apocryphal works.

52 *The Works of Saint Cyril of Jerusalem* (trans. Leo P. McCauley and Anthony A. Stephenson; Washington, D.C.: Catholic University of America, 1970) 2.45. See Aphrahat (b. last half of third century), *Dem.* 8.21–22; NPNF 13.381. Regarding judgment, Aphrahat says that retribution shall take place at the end, "when the Shepherd divides His flock and sets some on His right hand and some on His left... (Matt 25:32ff.). The Shepherd has not as yet divided His flock." Though the explicit reference here is to the First Gospel, this passage nevertheless demonstrates the use of pastoral language in an eschatological context.

Companion and ally...who among men wast crucified for many, who didst descend into Hades with great power, the sight of whom the princes of death did not endure, and thou didst ascend with great glory, and gathering all those who took refuge in thee thou didst prepare a way, and in thy footsteps they all journeyed whom thou didst redeem, and thou didst bring them to thine own flock and unite them with thy sheep.[53]

A similar use of pastoral language is evident in the following quotation from the *Epistula Apostolorum*:

And since those who slept [i.e., the dead] did not fulfil my commandment, they will be outside the kingdom and the fold of the shepherd [citation of John 10:1f.] and whomever remains outside the fold will the wolf eat (*Epis. Apos.* 44).[54]

In these examples we see that at times Christ and the resurrected dead are described as shepherd and sheep.

Early Christian literature also contains references to the figure of the gatekeeper, who guards the gates of Hades, at times acting as the agent of the ruler of the netherworld. In the *Gospel of Nicodemus*, an apocryphal work which has been dated to the early to mid-second century C.E.,[55] Hades, Lord of the underworld, cautions his gatekeepers, the demons: "Make fast well and strongly the gates of brass and the bars of iron, and hold my locks, and stand upright and watch every point."

In some cases, Christ gains entry to the netherworld by forcing the gate to open; in others, the gatekeeper simply opens the gate to him, recognizing his

---

[53] Edgar Hennecke and Wilhelm Schneemelcher, *New Testament Apocrypha* (trans. R. Mcl. Wilson; 2 vols.; Philadelphia: Westminster, 1963–65) 2.524. According to G. Bornkamm, this work is a Gnostic-Christian variety of Hellenistic-Oriental romance, belonging to the collection of apocryphal Acts. It was probably composed in the first half of the third century. See Hennecke, *Apocrypha*, 2.425–41. See also *The Acts of Judas Thomas*, in William Wright, *Apocryphal Acts of The Apostles edited from Syriac Manuscripts* (2 vols.; London, 1871, reprinted Amsterdam: Philo, 1968) 2.288, whose version reads as follows: "And Judas began to pray and to speak thus:...'Thou didst descend into Sheol with mighty power, and the dead saw Thee and became alive, and the Lord of death was not able to bear (it); and Thou didst ascend with great glory, and didst take up with Thee all who sought refuge with Thee, and didst tread for them the path (leading) up on high, and in Thy footsteps all Thy redeemed followed; and Thou didst bring them into Thy fold, and mingle them with Thy sheep.' "

[54] Hennecke, *Apocrypha*, 1.223.

[55] This work may be dated as early as the first half of the second century C.E. See Hennecke, *Apocrypha*, 1.447.

divine right to entry. In the *Nisibene Hymns* of Ephraem Syrus (fourth century C.E.), we read that

> Satan came with his servants, that he might see our Lord cast into Sheol, and might rejoice with Death his Counsellor; and he saw Him sorrowful and mourning....Death opened the gates of Sheol, and there shone from it the splendour of the face of our Lord; and like the men of Sodom they were smitten; they groped and sought the gate of Sheol, which they had lost (*Carm. Nis.* 41.15–16; NPNF 13.205).

In this passage, Satan is the overlord of the underworld, with Death as his gatekeeper. Death opens the gate to let Christ, the Light, come into the Netherworld.

This act on the part of Death is attributed by St. Cyril of Jerusalem to Death's fear:

> Death was panic-stricken on seeing a new visitant descending into the nether world, One not subject to the bonds of the place. Why, O you porters of hell, were you terrified on seeing Him? What unaccustomed fear seized upon you? Death fled away and his flight convicted him of cowardice.[56]

In a similar vein, Athanasius (fourth century) writes:

> Nor is it lawful to say that the Lord was in terror, at whom the keepers of hell's gates shuddered (cf. Job 38:17 [LXX]), and set open hell, and the graves did gape, and many bodies of the saints arose and appeared to their people (*C. Ar.* 3.29.56; NPNF 4.424).

That Christ opened the gates of hell, or caused them to be opened by the gatekeepers, is mentioned explicitly by several authors. Eusebius of Caesarea (late third, early fourth century) expounds Ps 22:11ff. in the following way:

> None of the angels ventured to enter Hades with Christ in His mission to succour souls. To Him only were the gates of Death opened, the doorkeepers of Hades saw and feared him, and he who has the power of Death, descending from his throne, spoke gently to Him with prayer and supplication.[57]

---

56 St. Cyril of Jerusalem, in *Works*, 2.44; see also PG 33.331–1181.
57 As quoted in MacCulloch, *Harrowing of Hell*, 111.

Then Christ shattered the gates of brass, broke the iron bonds, and set free the prisoners from Hades.[58] For Eusebius, as for Cyril, Death is the Lord of the Underworld, and his agents the doorkeepers.

In the *Acts of Judas Thomas*, Christ is told: "...Thou didst descend to Sheol, and go to its uttermost end; and didst open its gates, and bring out its prisoners, and didst treat for them the path (leading) above by the nature of Thy Godhead."[59] Finally, in the *Odes of Solomon* 42:17, the dead ask Christ to "open for us the door by which we may come out to Thee; For we perceive that our death does not touch Thee."[60]

In the above passages, we have seen that the figure of the gatekeeper, who is different from the lord of the underworld, and the gates which he keeps, are prominent in the Christian descent passages. Similarly important is the Voice of Christ. In the *paroimia* the voice of the shepherd, by which he calls the name of the sheep, is heard by them and has a role in their departure from the sheepfold. In the following descent passages, the Voice calls the gates to open, preaches to the dead, bursts the graves, and raises the dead, who, like the sheep of 10:1–5, hear the voice. In the *Gospel of Nicodemus*, we are told that

> while Satan and Hades were speaking...to one another, a loud voice like thunder sounded: "Lift up your gates, O rulers, and be lifted up, O everlasting doors, and the King of glory shall come in" (Ps 24:7; 23:7 [LXX]) When Hades heard this, he said to Satan, Go out, if you can, and withstand him....[61]

Not only Hades but also the dead in his netherworld heard his voice. That Christ preached in the netherworld is suggested in 1 Peter 3:19, and picked up by many Church Fathers. For example, Justin Martyr (second century C.E.) said that "The Lord God remembered His dead people of Israel who lay in their graves, and He descended to preach to them His salvation."[62]

Clement of Alexandria (late second, early third century C.E.) develops this point at length. In the *Stromata* he declares that "those in Hades (outside the Law) hear the voice of the Lord. We have not seen his form but we have heard his voice." He continues:

---

[58] Ibid.

[59] Wright, *Acts*, 2.155.

[60] J. H. Charlesworth, ed., *The Odes of Solomon* (Oxford: Clarendon, 1973) 146. This work is a Gnostic hymn book from the second century. See Hennecke, *Apocrypha*, 2.809, and *Odes*, vii.

[61] Hennecke, *Apocrypha*, 1.473.

[62] Justin Martyr, *Dial.* 72; ANCL 2.189. See also Irenaeus, *Adv. haer.* 4.22.1; ANCL 2.467.

Wherefore the Lord preached the Gospel to those in Hades. Accordingly the Scripture says, "Hades says to Destruction, We have not seen His form, but we have heard His voice." (Job 28:22). It is not plainly the place, which, the words above say, heard the voice, but those who have been put in Hades, and have abandoned themselves to destruction...They, then, are those that hear the divine power and voice...But how? Do not [the Scriptures] show that the Lord preached the Gospel to those that perished in the flood, or rather had been chained, and to those kept "in ward and guard" (1 Pet 3:19, 20)? And it has been shown also, in the second book of the *Stromata*, that the apostles, following the Lord, preach the Gospel to those in Hades....If, then, the Lord descended to Hades for no other end but to preach the Gospel, as He did descend; it was either to preach the Gospel to all or the Hebrews only....[63]

The image of Christ's voice in hell recurs several times in the hymns of Ephraem Syrus. In Hymn 36.11, he says: "...the voice of our Lord sounded into Hell, and He cried aloud and burst the graves one by one." Hymn 37.8 asks: "And who is he then that shall bear for me all these things, that I shall see Sheol left alone, because this voice which has rent the graves, makes her desolate and sends forth the dead that were in her midst?" In Hymn 41.15, Satan saw Death "sorrowful and mourning because of the dead who at the voice of the Firstborn, lived and came forth thence even from Sheol."[64] The context makes it clear that Christ is in Hades.

The great power of the voice of Christ in Hades is described in the *Acts of Judas Thomas:*

And thou didst show the glory of Thy Godhead in Thy longsuffering towards our manhood, when Thou didst hurl the evil (one) from his power, and didst call with Thy voice to the dead, and they became alive; and to those who were alive and hoping in Thee, Thou didst promise an inheritance in Thy kingdom.[65]

---

[63] *Strom.* 6.6; ANF 2.490. In *Strom.* 2.9, he refers to the apostles' preaching as well as the question of whether the apostles descended alive or dead. He also refers to the Shepherd of Hermas, who says in a similar fashion: "when they fell asleep in the power and faith of the Son of God, the Apostles and teachers, who proclaimed the name of the Son of God, preached also to those who had previously fallen asleep and themselves gave to them the seal of the proclamation." This Jewish-Christian work can be dated to the early second century. See *Shepherd of Hermas*, Sim. 9.15, 16; ANF 2.49.

[64] *Carm. Nis.* 36.11, 37.8, 41.15; see NPNF 13.197, 199, 205.

[65] Wright, *Acts*, 2.154.

Similar is Aphrahat's description of Resurrection:

> ...with one word of summons He will cause all the end (of the world) to hear, and all that are laid (in the grave) shall leap forth and rise up; and no word shall return void to Him that sent it forth...and this is the voice through whom the dead shall live.[66]

In these passages, therefore, the voice of Christ is seen as the instrument through which he managed to enter the gates of hell, as well as to preach to and resurrect the dead.[67]

In other passages, the dead do not leave their graves peacefully, but rather appear to be ejected forcibly. For example, in the Greek version of the *Gospel of Nicodemus* Hades says:

> Behold, I see that all those whom I have swallowed up from the beginning of the world are disquieted. I have pain in the stomach. Lazarus who was snatched from me before seems to me no good sign. For not like a dead man, but like an eagle he flew away from me, so quickly did the earth cast him out [ἔξω ἔρριψε]. Therefore I adjure you by your gifts and mine, do not bring him here. For I believe that he comes here to raise all the dead. And I tell you this: By the darkness which surrounds us, if you bring him here, none of the dead will be left for me.[68]

The story continues:

> While Hades was thus speaking with Satan, the King of glory stretched out his right hand, and took hold of our forefather Adam and raised him up. Then he turned also to the rest and said: Come with me, all you who have suffered death through the tree which this man touched.

---

[66] *Dem.* 8.16; NPNF 13.380. In this passage there is a direct citation of John 5:25.

[67] Other examples are to be found in the *Odes of Solomon*, for example, 31:6–7, in which Christ says, "Come forth, you who have been afflicted, and receive joy And possess yourselves through grace; and take unto you to immortal life." See *Odes*, 116.

[68] Hennecke, *Apocrypha*, 1.473. Very similar is the *Homily on the Devil and Hades* which parallels these two passages, quoted in MacCulloch, *Harrowing of Hell*, 177 and 180: "Hades says: 'If He comes, He will cast forth those in my keeping.'" Then he describes how Lazarus' body became corrupt, and how Christ came to his door and called Lazarus forth. "He sprang forth from my belly, as a lion swift from a den on its prey, as an eagle he leaped forth, all weakness laid aside in the twinkling of an eye."

For behold, I raise you all up again through the tree of the cross. With that he put them all out [πρὸς ταῦτα ἐξέβαλεν ἀπάντας ἔξω].[69]

In the *Homily on the Devil and Hades*, attributed to Eusebius of Alexandria (fifth century?), Hades warns:

Go and do as thou wilt. Wage battle, and if thou overcome Him, we shall shut Him up here, and thou shalt reign over the Jews. But if thou art conquered, He cometh and casteth out [ἐκβάλει/ἐκβάλλει][70] whom I have shut up, and then He will bind thee and thy servants the Jews and will deliver you to me, and with you we shall be wretched.[71]

A similar idea is expressed in the *Homily on the Passion, for the Preparation Day* (falsely attributed to John Chrysostom):

John said, "Did not I tell you that he will come and cast you out [ἔρχεται καὶ ἐκβάλλει]?"...Then the Lord, taking all the prophets, thrust them forth [ἐξέβαλεν] out of Hades, saying, "Go into Paradise," and they rejoicing, sprang forth from Hades.[72]

In these passages, the departure from the netherworld is expressed using rather violent language, as a casting forth, done by Christ himself, or by the earth in which the dead have been entombed. This idea is a striking parallel to our *paroimia*, in which the rather unusual term ἐκβάλλειν—to cast out—is used to describe the act by which Jesus takes out "his own" from the sheepfold. In the context of the *paroimia* commentators usually translate the verb weakly, as "led out,"[73] but its usage in the Synoptic Gospels is more violent, referring particularly to the casting out of demons (Matt 7:22 and parallels), the throwing of people into the outer darkness (Matt 8:12 and parallels), or ejecting people from a room (Matt 9:25 and parallels). As we see in the above examples, it is

---

69 Hennecke, *Apocrypha*, 1.475. For Greek, see K. V. Tischendorf, ed., *Evangelia Apocrypha* (1876; reprinted Hildesheim: Georg Olms, 1966) 330.

70 See PG 86.402, in which there are three variants of this text, in two of which the word ἐκβάλλει, or ἐκβάλει, appears.

71 MacCulloch, *Harrowing of Hell*, 179–80.

72 See PG 62.723–24. A similar idea is expressed in the *Odes of Solomon* 42:11, in which the writer says, "Sheol saw me and was shattered. And Death ejected me and many with me"; see *Odes*, 145.

73 S.v. ἐκβάλλω, BAGD. See also Simonis, 177, who sees this verb as an indicator of the liberation from the temple of Judaism, and Schnackenburg (Schnack. 2.282, n. 28), who argues against this viewpoint.

used in these post–New Testament passages to refer to the way in which the dead leave their tombs in the earth.

Finally, there are some descent passages in which the pattern of movement parallels that attributed to the shepherd in John 10:1–5. The sheep are in an enclosure, the shepherd enters, calls them, and leads them out of the enclosure. This pattern is implicit in all of the examples of the κατάβασις which we have looked at. It comes to explicit expression in the Apostles' Creed as cited above as well as in the *Acts of Thomas*. This text describes Christ as the

> Son of the living God, the undaunted power which overthrew the enemy, the voice that was heard by the archons, which shook all their powers; ambassador sent from the height who didst descend even to Hell, who having opened the doors didst bring up thence those who for many ages had been shut up in the treasury of darkness, and show them the way that leads up to the height.[74]

This passage presents a clear parallel to the shepherd entering the fold and leading the sheep out.

There are also several images or incidents from the context of the *paroimia* to which the descent passages refer directly. The first is the image of Jesus as the door (John 10:7, 9). In his second homily to 1 Kings, Origen (second to third century) explains:

> Since all descended to Hades before Christ, so the prophets were His forerunners. The souls of those that slept were in need of the prophetic grace, preaching Christ's sojourn in Hades. Before the coming of my Lord Jesus Christ none could pass beyond where the tree of life was, and the appointed guards of the way to it. Neither Samuel nor Abraham, who was seen by Dives in Abraham's Bosom, could pass the flaming sword. Therefore the patriarchs and prophets and all waited the coming of my Lord Jesus Christ, that He might open the way, for "I am the Way," "I am the Door." The way to the tree of life is, that if thou passest through the fire, the flame may not burn thee.[75]

---

[74] Hennecke, *Apocrypha*, 2.448.

[75] The translation is that of MacCulloch, *Harrowing*, 104. See PG 12.1026. A similar idea is expressed in *Odes of Solomon* 17:9–11 (*Odes*, 75), "And from there He gave me the way of His steps; and I opened the doors which were closed. And I shattered the bars of iron, For my own shackles had grown hot and melted before me. And nothing appeared closed to me; because I was the opening of everything. And I went towards all my bondsmen to loose them..."

The second direct reference to the context of 10:1–5 concerns the raising of Lazarus, which is recounted in chapter 11 of the Fourth Gospel. To the passages we have already looked at which refer to this event may be added the poignant lament of Sheol, as imagined by Ephraem Syrus:

> Sheol...wept for Lazarus when he went forth, "Go in peace thou dead that livest, bewailed by two houses of mourning." Within and without were lamentations for him; for his sisters wept for him when he came into the grave unto me, and I wept for him as he went forth. In his death there was weeping among the living; likewise in Sheol is great mourning at his resurrection (*Carm. Nis.* 37.6; NPNF 13.198).

In Hymn 41.12–16, the Evil one says:

> 12. For He who brought Lazarus to life though dead, how can Death suffice against Him?
> 13. Death says: O raiser of the dead to life where art thou! Thou shalt be to me for meat, instead of the sweet Lazarus, whose savour lo! It is still in my mouth...
> 16. Three days have passed for him, and let us say to him, O thou of three days, who didst raise Lazarus, when he had lain four days, raise thine own self. Death opened the gates of Sheol, and there shone from it the splendour of the face of our lord (*Carm. Nis.* 41; NPNF 13.205).

Another parallel in this literature to the context of our *paroimia* is found in the use of the darkness and light motif. As in the classical Greek literature and the Egyptian Book of the Dead,[76] in the patristic literature and the New Testament Apocrypha, darkness is associated with death and Hades, light with life and resurrection. For example, the *Gospel of Nicodemus* relates that

> At the hour of midnight there rose upon the darkness there something like the light of the sun and shone, and light fell upon us all, and we saw one another.. This shining comes from a great light. The prophet Isaiah...said: "This shining comes from the Father and the Son and the Holy Spirit..." After the crashing of the gates, the gospel proclaims, "The King of glory entered in like a man, and all the dark places of Hades were illumined."[77]

---

[76] Zandee, *Death*, 88–89.
[77] Hennecke, *Apocrypha*, 1.474.

With an introductory formula reminiscent of John 10:1, Jesus in the Greek recension of the *Epistula Apostolorum* declares:

> Truly I say to you, as the Father awakened me from the dead, in the same manner you also will arise in the flesh, and he will cause you to rise up above the heavens to the place of which I have spoken to you from the beginning which he who sent me has prepared for you...
>
> Truly I say to you that I have received all power from my Father that I may bring back those in darkness into light and those in corruptibility into incorruptibility and those in error into righteousness and those in death into life, and that those in captivity may be loosed....I am...the resurrection of the dead (*Epis. Apos.* 21).[78]

Finally, Aphrahat connects the imagery explicitly with resurrection, saying that Death heard God say to Moses "that God is King of the Dead and the living, and that it is appointed to the children of Adam to come forth from his darkness and arise with their bodies" (*Dem.* 22.2; NPNF 13.402).

These quotations indicate that the contrast of light and darkness, while occurring in the natural world and needing little explanation, is also used to describe the contrast between life and death, and especially the association between darkness and death, and light and eternal life. This is an association which pervades the Fourth Gospel and plays a major role in both of the chapters which frame chapter 10: chapter 9 revolves around this contrast, coupled with the contrast between sight and blindness, and chapter 11 introduces the raising of Lazarus episode using similar language.

No hard and fast conclusions should be drawn from the similarities in language and narrative structure between these post–New Testament examples of the descent motif and our *paroimia* in John 10:1–5. Their later date precludes their use by the evangelist as sources for his gospel. These similarities do, however, raise the possibility that the *paroimia* may have been read by some second–century and subsequent Christian readers as a reference to Jesus' descent, and as such may itself have influenced the specific formulations of the descent motif in the New Testament Apocrypha and patristic literature. In support of this point, we may note that direct reference to 10:7, 9 is made in some of the descent passages. In fact, as Johannes Quasten has discussed in detail, the Good Shepherd image for Christ is one which appears frequently on sarcophagi and in

---

[78] Ibid., 1.205–6.

sepulchral art and medallions in the first few centuries of the common era.[79] He argues that the Good Shepherd was seen as offering protection from the devil and his demons for the souls of the dead on their journey to the heavenly realm,[80] just as the good shepherd offers protection from the wolves according to John 10.[81] Furthermore, Quasten suggests that the opposition of the Good Shepherd to demonic forces has its roots in the Fourth Gospel (e.g., 10:28)[82] and ties in to the descent motif as it is expressed in Col 2:15 and Phil 2:10.[83] Finally, he suggests, based on Justin's *Dialogue with Trypho* 69.3 and 64.7 (cf. also *Apologia* 1.54), that early Christians made an explicit connection between Heracles, who conquered wild beasts and descended to the netherworld, and the Good Shepherd.[84]

These examples, and Quasten's analysis, point to the explicit association of the Good Shepherd imagery and the καΤάβασις motif in the early centuries of the Christian church. This implies that at least some readers were interpreting the *paroimia* in its Johannine context as an allusion to Jesus' descent. The pre-Christian linking of pastoral language and the καΤάβασις motif suggests that the latter may have been a part of the extrinsic data which implied readers would have brought to bear on their reading of the *paroimia*.

CONCLUSION

Although our survey of extra-Johannine literature is by no means complete, the passages that we have looked at indicate that both in the classical Greek literature as well as in the later patristic and Christian apocryphal literature, there are connections between pastoral language and the motif of the hero's descent into hell. None of these passages likely served as a source for our *paroimia*, but the coming together of these motifs is suggestive. Also relevant may have been the use of pastoral language to describe the relationship between a king and his subjects, as well as that between the redeemer and the redeemed, the one who resurrects and those that are resurrected. These associations are of

---

[79] For examples, translations, and detailed discussion, see Johannes Quasten, "Der Gute Hirte in Frühchristlicher Totenliturgie und Grabeskunst," *Miscellanea Giovanni Mercati* (vol. 1, Studi e Testi 121; Citta del Vaticano: Biblioteca Apostolica Vaticana, 1946) 373–406.

[80] Ibid., 396, 412.

[81] Ibid., 403.

[82] Ibid., 376. It is interesting to note, however, that there is no mention of the association of the "Good Shepherd" and death in his later article on John 10 (see note 79 above). One may speculate that in the latter case, his purpose was to demonstrate the authenticity of the *paroimia* and hence there was no room to argue for such associations.

[83] Ibid., 396.

[84] Ibid., 378–80.

course consistent with New Testament christology in general, and Johannine christology in particular. For the Fourth Evangelist, Jesus is the divinely-sent King whose jurisdiction and power extend over the world of both the living and the dead.

Tempting as are the parallels between the *paroimia* and the κατάβασις passages, it would be hasty to conclude that John 10:1–5 was understood by the implied reader as a passage depicting Jesus' descent to the underworld. Although the Johannine Jesus is portrayed as calling the dead from the tomb (5:24–29; 11:43–44), there is no hint in the gospel of a belief in his physical descent to the netherworld between the time of his death and his resurrection. Nevertheless, the description of the sheepfold as a place of death[85] from which the dead believers—Jesus' own sheep—are led forth by their shepherd is not inconsistent with the cosmological tale. In this strand of the gospel, as we have argued in chapter two, the "world" apart from Jesus is in the grips of darkness, sin, and death, and the inhabitants of this world are dead unless they believe in Jesus as the Christ, the Son of God, sent by God into the world to do God's will. In believing, they also follow him out of the world, pass from death to life, as do the dead in their tombs in the κατάβασις passages in early Christian literature. Hence, despite the absence of evidence regarding Johannine belief in Jesus' physical descent, the parallels in language and structure between the κατάβασις passages and the Johannine *paroimia*, as well as the appropriateness of the descent motif in the context of the cosmological tale, leave open the possibility of reading the *paroimia* as an allusion to the κατάβασις of Jesus. Such a reading adds yet another level to the reader's encounter with this passage, alongside the historical, ecclesiological, and cosmological readings discussed in the earlier chapters of this study.

---

[85] According to the *Thesaurus Graecae Linguae* (ed. Henrico Stephanus [Paris: Ambrosius Firmin Didot, 1831–56], s.v. αὐλή), αὐλή in its most general sense simply refers to an enclosure like a closed courtyard. Although it is used to refer to a place where sheep and other animals are kept, its meaning is not exclusively connected to this use. This would support what we have found to be the case in the interpretation of the αὐλή in John 10:1–5, namely that the meaning of αὐλή in this passage derives from its context in the *paroimia* and from the interpretations given to the other elements. While I did not come across any Greek examples in which αὐλή clearly refers to the "tomb" or netherworld, there is an interesting example in which the αὐλή is the place to which the heads of the damned are led. Suidas, *Suidae Lexicon*, part 1 (ed. Ada Adler; Leipzig: B. G. Teubner, 1928) s.v. αὐλή.

BIBLIOGRAPHY

PRIMARY SOURCES

Classical Literature.

Apollodorus, *Biblioteca*. Loeb Classical Library. 1976.

Aristotle. *Aristotle's Poetics*. Trans. Kenneth A. Telford. New York: University Press of America, 1961.

Euripedes. *Hercules*. Ed. Kevin Hargreaves Lee. Leipzig: B. G. Teubner, 1988.

Euripides. *Alcestis*. In *The Complete Greek Tragedies*, vol. 3. Ed. D. Grene and R. Lattimore. Chicago; University of Chicago Press, 1955.

Homer. *The Odyssey*. Trans. E. Rieu. Harmondsworth, Middlesex: Penguin, 1946.

Pindar. *The Odes of Pindar*. Trans. Geoffrey S. Conway. London: J. M. Dent, 1972.

Seneca, *Seneca's Tragedies*. 2 vols. LCL. 1929–38.

Suidas. *Suidae Lexicon*. Ed. Ada Adler. Leipzig: B. G. Teubner, 1928.

Virgil. *Aeneid: Book Six*. Ed. H. E. Gould and J. E. Whiteley. London: Macmillan, 1946.

Apocryphal Literature.

Charlesworth, J. H., ed. *The Odes of Solomon*. Oxford: Clarendon, 1973.

Hennecke,Edgar, and Wilhelm Schneemelcher, eds. *New Testament Apocrypha*. Trans. R. Mcl. Wilson. 2 vols. Philadelphia: Westminster, 1963–5.

Tischendorf, K. V., ed. *Evangelia Apocrypha*. 1876. Reprinted Hildesheim: Georg Olms, 1966.

Wright, William, ed. *Apocryphal Acts of The Apostles edited from Syriac Manuscripts*. London, 1871. Reprinted Amsterdam: Philo, 1968.

Patristic Sources.

Aphrahat, *Select Demonstrations*. In *Nicene and Post-Nicene Fathers*, 2d series, vol. 12, part 2. New York: Parker and Co., 1898.

Athanasius, *Discourses against the Arians*. In *Nicene and Post-Nicene Fathers*, 2d series, vol. 5. Grand Rapids: Eerdmans, 1891.

Augustine. *Lectures or Tractates on the Gospel According to John*. vol. 2. In *The Works of Aurelius Augustine*, vol. 11. Ed. Marcus Dods, trans. James Innes. Edinburgh: T. and T. Clark, 1874.

Chrysostom, John. *Homilies on the Gospel of St. John*. In *Nicene and Post-Nicene Fathers*, vol. 14. Grand Rapids: Eerdmans, 1956.

Clement of Alexandria. *Stromata*. In *Ante-Nicene Fathers*, vol. 2. New York: Scribners, 1903.

Cyril. *The Works of Saint Cyril of Jerusalem*, vol. 2. Trans. Leo P. McCauley and Anthony A. Stephenson. Washington, D.C.: Catholic University of America, 1970.

Justin Martyr. *Dialogue with Trypho*. In *Ante-Nicene Christian Library*. Ed. A. Roberts and J. Donaldson, vol. 2. Trans. Marcus Dods et al. Edinburgh: T. and T. Clark, 1868.

Irenaeus, *Against Heresies*. In *Ante-Nicene Christian Library*, vol. 5. Trans. A. Roberts, J. Donaldson. Edinburgh: T. and T. Clark, 1869.

Shepherd of Hermas. In *The Apostolic Fathers*, vol. 6. Ed. Gradon F. Snyder. London: Nelson, 1968.

Tyrannius Rufinus. *A Commentary on the Apostles' Creed*. Trans. J. N. D. Kelly. New York: Newman, 1954.

Other Sources.

Philo of Alexandria. *Philo*. Loeb Classical Library, 10 vols. London and Cambridge, Mass., 1929–62.

SECONDARY SOURCES

Literary Theory.

Abrams, M. H. *A Glossary of Literary Terms.* 3rd ed. New York: Holt, Rinehart and Winston, 1971.

Chatman, Seymour. *Story and Discourse: Narrative Structure in Fiction and Film.* Ithaca: Cornell University Press, 1978.

Eagleton, Terry. *Literary Theory: An Introduction.* Oxford: Basil Blackwell, 1983.

Egan, Kieran. "What is a Plot?" *New Literary History* 9 (1978) 455–73.

Fish, Stanley. *Is there a Text in this Class?* Cambridge: Harvard University Press, 1980.

Fowler, Roger, ed. *A Dictionary of Modern Critical Terms.* London: Routledge and Kegan Paul, 1973.

Frye, Northrop et al., eds. *The Harper Handbook to Literature.* New York: Harper and Row, 1985.

Genette, Gérard. *Narrative Discourse: An Essay in Method.* Ithaca: Cornell University, 1980.

Holman, C. Hugh. *A Handbook to Literature.* New York: Macmillan, 1986.

Iser, Wolfgang. "The Reading Process: A Phenomenological Approach." In Tompkins, *Reader-Response,* 52–57.

————. *The Implied Reader.* Baltimore: The Johns Hopkins University Press, 1974.

Jauss, Hans Robert. "Literary History as a Challenge to Literary Theory." *New Literary History* 2 (1970–71) 7–31.

————. "Theses on the Transition from the Aesthetics of Literary Works to a Theory of Aesthetic Experience." In Valdés, *Interpretation,* 137–47.

Mailloux, Stephen. "Learning to Read: Interpretation and Reader-Response Criticism." *Studies in the Literary Imagination* 12 (1979) 93–108.

————. *Rhetorical Power*. Ithaca: Cornell University Press, 1989.

Prince, Gerald. "Introduction to the Study of the Narratee." In Tompkins, *Reader-Response*, 7–25.

Tompkins, Jane P. *Reader-Response Criticism: From Formalism to Post-structuralism*. Baltimore: The Johns Hopkins University Press, 1980.

Valdés, Mario J., and Owen Miller, eds. *The Identity of the Literary Text*. Toronto: University of Toronto, 1985.

————, and Owen Miller, ed. *Interpretation of Narrative*. Toronto: University of Toronto, 1978.

Commentaries on the Gospel of John

Barrett, C. K. *The Gospel According to St. John*. 2d ed. Philadelphia: Westminster, 1978.

Bernard, J. H. *A Critical and Exegetical Commentary on the Gospel According to St. John*. Vol. 2. Edinburgh: T. and T. Clark, 1928.

Brown, R. E. *The Gospel According to John*. 2 vols. The Anchor Bible, 29–29A. New York: Doubleday, 1966–70.

Bultmann, Rudolf. *The Gospel of John*. Philadelphia: Westminster, 1971.

Carson, D. A. *The Gospel According to John*. Grand Rapids: Eerdmans, 1991.

Godet, F. *Commentary on the Gospel of St. John*. Vol. 2. 3rd ed. Edinburgh: T. and T. Clark, 1892.

Haenchen, Ernst. *John 1: A Commentary on the Gospel of John Chapter 1–6*. Philadelphia: Fortress, 1984.

Hoskyns, E. C., and F. N. Davey. *The Fourth Gospel*. London: Faber and Faber, 1947.

Kysar, Robert. *John's Story of Jesus*. Philadelphia: Fortress, 1984.

Lightfoot, R. G. *St. John's Gospel*. London: Oxford University Press, 1956.

Lindars, Barnabas. *The Gospel of John*. The New Century Bible Commentary. Grand Rapids: Eerdmans, 1972.

Odeberg, Hugo. *The Fourth Gospel.* Uppsala, 1929. Reprinted Amsterdam: B.R. Grüner, 1968.

Schlatter, Adolf. *Der Evangelist Johannes.* 3rd. ed. Stuttgart: Calwer Verlag, 1960.

Schnackenburg, Rudolf. *The Gospel According to St. John.* 3 vols. New York: Crossroad, 1980–82.

Strack, Hermann, and Paul Billerbeck. *Kommentar zum NT aus Talmud und Midrasch.* Vol. 2. München: Beck, 1924.

Wellhausen, Julius. *Das Evangelium Johannis.* Berlin: Georg Reimer, 1908.

Zahn, T. *Das Evangelium des Johannes ausgelegt.* Leipzig: A. Deichert, 1908.

Other Books and Articles

Alter, Robert. *The Art of Biblical Narrative.* New York: Basic Books, 1981.

Ashton, John. "The Transformation of Wisdom: A Study of the Prologue of John's Gospel." *NTS* 32 (1986) 161–86.

———. ed. *The Interpretation of John.* Issues in Religion and Theology 9. Philadelphia: Fortress, 1986.

———. *Understanding the Fourth Gospel.* Oxford: Clarendon, 1991.

Baird, J. Arthur. *The Justice of God in the Teaching of Jesus.* Philadelphia: Westminster, 1963.

Bassler, Jouette M. "Mixed Signals: Nicodemus in the Fourth Gospel." *JBL* 108 (1989) 635–46.

Beutler, Johannes, and Robert T. Fortna, eds. *The Shepherd Discourse of John 10 and its Context.* SNTSMS 67. Cambridge: Cambridge University Press, 1991.

Black, Matthew, ed. *The Book of Enoch or I Enoch: A New English Edition.* Leiden: Brill, 1985.

Blank, Josef. *Krisis: Untersuchungen zur johanneischen Christologie und Eschatologie.* Freiburg: Lambertus, 1964.

Boomershine, Thomas. *Story Journey: An Invitation to the Gospel as Storytelling.* Nashville: Abingdon, 1988.

Borgen, Peder. "God's Agent in the Fourth Gospel." In *Religions in Antiquity*, ed. Jacob Neusner, 67–78. Leiden: Brill, 1968.

Brown, Raymond E. *The Community of the Beloved Disciple.* New York: Paulist, 1979.

———. "Other Sheep Not of This Fold: The Johannine Perspective on Christian Diversity in the Late First Century." *JBL* 97 (1978) 5–22.

———. "Parable and Allegory Reconsidered." *NovT* 5 (1962) 36–45.

Bruns, J. E. "The Discourse on the Good Shepherd and the Rite of Ordination." *AER* 149 (1963) 386–391.

Bultmann, Rudolf. *Theology of the New Testament.* Vol. 2. New York: Charles Scribner's Sons, 1955.

Caird, G. B. *The Language and Imagery of the Bible.* London: Duckworth, 1980.

Carson, D. A. "The Purpose of the Fourth Gospel: John 20:31 Reconsidered." *JBL* 106 (1987) 639–51.

———. "Understanding and Misunderstanding in the Fourth Gospel." *TynBul* 33 (1982) 59–91.

———. *Divine Sovereignty and Human Responsibility.* Atlanta: John Knox, 1981.

Coetzee, C. J. "Christ and the Prince of this World in the Gospel and the Epistles of St. John." *Neot* 2 (1968) 104–21.

Cooper, Alan. "Ps 24:7–10: Mythology and Exegesis." *JBL* 102 (1983) 37–60.

Croon, Johan Harm. *The Herdsman of the Dead: Studies on some cults, myths and legends of the ancient Greek colonization-area.* Utrecht: Drukkerij S. Budde, 1952.

Culpepper, R. Alan. *Anatomy of the Fourth Gospel.* Philadelphia: Fortress, 1983.

De Jonge, Marinus. *Jesus: Stranger from Heaven and Son of God.* SBLSBS 11. Missoula: Scholars Press, 1977.

De la Potterie, Ignace. "C'est lui qui a ouvert la voie: la finale du prologue johannique." *Bib* 69 (1988) 340–70.

———. "The Truth in Saint John." In Ashton, *Interpretation*, 53–66. Philadelphia: Fortress, 1986. Originally appeared as "La Verita in San Giovanni." *RivB* 11 (1963) 3–24.

Derrett, J. Duncan M. "The Good Shepherd: St. John's Use of Jewish Halakah and Haggadah." *ST* 27 (1973) 25–50.

Dewey, Kim E. "*Paroimia* in the Gospel of John." *Semeia* 17 (1980) 81–100.

Dodd, C. H. *The Interpretation of the Fourth Gospel*. Cambridge: Cambridge University Press, 1953.

———. *The Parables of the Kingdom*. Glasgow: Fontana, 1961.

Du Rand, Jan A. "A syntactical and narratological reading of John 10 in coherence with chapter 9." In Beutler and Fortna, *Shepherd Discourse*, 94–115.

Duke, Paul D. *Irony in the Fourth Gospel*. Atlanta: John Knox, 1985.

Farnell, L. R. *Greek Hero Cults and Ideas of Immortality*. Oxford: Clarendon, 1921.

Fink, Josef. "Heracles Held und Heiland." *Antike und Abendland* 9 (1960) 73–79.

Fiorenza, Elisabeth Schüssler. *In Memory of Her*. New York: Crossroad, 1983.

Fischer, Karl Martin. "Der johanneische Christus und der gnostische Erlöser." In *Gnosis und Neues Testament*, ed. Karl-Wolfgang Troeger, 235–66. Berlin: Gerd Mohn, 1973.

George, Augustin. "Je suis la porte des brebis." *BVC* 51 (1963) 21.

Glasson, T. F. *Moses in the Fourth Gospel*. London: SCM, 1963.

Guilding, Aileen. *The Fourth Gospel and Jewish Worship*. Oxford: Clarendon, 1960.

Hofbeck, Sebald. σημεῖον. Wurzburg: Vier Türme, 1966.

Jaeger, Werner. *Early Christianity and Greek Paideia*. London: Oxford University Press, 1961.

Jeremias, Joachim. *The Parables of Jesus*. Rev. ed. London: SCM, 1972.

Johnson, Elizabeth A. "Jesus, the Wisdom of God: A Biblical Basis for a Non-Androcentric Christianity." *ETL* 61 (1985) 284–9.

Johnston, George. *The Spirit-Paraclete in the Gospel of John*. Cambridge: Cambridge University Press, 1970.

Jost, W. ποιμήν: *Das Bild vom Hirten in der biblischen Uberlieferung und seine christologische Bedeutung*. Giessen, 1939.

Jülicher, Adolf. *Die Gleichnisreden Jesu*. Vol. 2. Tübingen, 1910. Reprinted Darmstadt: Wissenschaftliche Buchgesellschaft, 1969.

Käsemann, Ernst. *The Testament of Jesus*. Philadelphia: Fortress, 1968.

Kermode, Frank. "John." In *The Literary Guide to the Bible*, ed. Robert Alter and Frank Kermode, 440–66. Cambridge: Harvard University Press, 1987.

Kiefer, Odo. *Die Hirtenrede*. Stuttgart: Verlag Katholisches Bibelwerk, 1967.

Kimelman, Reuven. "*Birkat Ha-Minim* and the Lack of Evidence for an Anti-Christian Jewish Prayer in Late Antiquity." In *Jewish and Christian Self-Definition*, vol. 2, ed. E. P. Sanders, 226–55, 351–403. Philadelphia: Fortress, 1981.

Kittel, Gerhard, and G. Friedrich, eds. *The Theological Dictionary of the New Testament*. Trans. G.W. Bromiley. 10 vols. Grand Rapids: Eerdmans, 1964–74.

Klauck, Hans-Josef. *Allegorie und Allegorese in synoptischen Gleichnistexten*. Neutestamentliche Abhandlungen 13. Münster: Aschendorff, 1978.

Knight, W. F. Jackson. *Vergil: Epic and Anthropology*. Ed. John. D. Christie. New York: Barnes and Noble, 1967.

Koester, Craig R. "'The Savior of the World' (John 4:42)." *JBL* 109 (1990) 665–80.

Kossen, H. B. "Who were the Greeks of John XII 20?" In *Studies in John: J. N. Sevenster Festschrift*, 97–110. Leiden: Brill, 1970.

Kroll, Josef. *Gott und Hölle: Der Mythos vom Descensuskampfe*. Leipzig: B. G. Teubner, 1932.

Kysar, Robert. "Johannine Metaphor—Meaning and Function: A Literary Case Study of John 10:1–18." *Semeia* 53 (1991) 81– 111.

————. *John, the Maverick Gospel*. Atlanta: John Knox, 1976.

————. *The Fourth Evangelist and his Gospel*. Minneapolis: Augsburg, 1975.

Leith, John. *Creeds of the Churches: A Reader in Christian Doctrine from the Bible to the Present*. Rev. ed. Richmond, Va.: John Knox, 1973.

Lindars, Barnabas. "The Apocalyptic Myth and the Death of Christ." *BJRL* 57 (1974–5) 366–87.

————. "The Son of Man in the Johannine Christology." In *Christ and Spirit in the New Testament*, ed. Barnabas Lindars and S. S. Smalley, 43–60. Cambridge: Cambridge University Press, 1974.

Linnemann, Eta. *Parables of Jesus: Introduction and Exposition*. London: SPCK, 1966.

MacCulloch, J. A. *The Harrowing of Hell: A Comparative Study of an Early Christian Doctrine*. Edinburgh: T. and T. Clark, 1930.

Manns, Fréderic. *L'Evangile de Jean à la lumière du Judaisme*. Studium Biblicum Franciscanum, Analecta 33. Jerusalem: Franciscan Printing Press, 1991.

Marrou, H. I. *A History of Education in Antiquity*. Trans. George Lamb. London: Sheed and Ward, 1956.

Martin, James P. "John 10:1–10." *Int* 32 (1978) 171–75.

Martyn, J. L. *History and Theology in the Fourth Gospel*. 2d ed. Nashville: Abingdon, 1979.

————. *The Gospel of John in Christian History*. New York: Paulist, 1978.

McKnight, Edgar V., ed. *Reader Perspectives on the New Testament*. *Semeia* 48 (1989).

Meeks, Wayne A. "The Man from Heaven in Johannine Sectarianism." *JBL* 91 (1972) 44–72.

————. *The Prophet-King: Moses Traditions and the Johannine Christology*. Leiden: Brill, 1967.

Meyer, Paul W. "A Note on John 10:1–18." *JBL* 75 (1956) 232–35.

Minear, Paul S. *John, The Martyr's Gospel*. New York: Pilgrims, 1984.

Moore, Stephen D. "Rifts in (a reading of) the fourth gospel, or: Does Johannine irony still collapse on a reading that draws attention to itself?" *Neot* 23 (1989) 5–17.

———. *Literary Criticism and the Gospels: The Theoretical Challenge*. New Haven: Yale University Press, 1989.

Nicholson, Godfrey C. *Death as Departure*. Chico, Calif.: Scholars Press, 1983.

O'Day, Gail R. *Revelation in the Fourth Gospel*. Philadelphia: Fortress, 1986.

Painter, John. "Tradition, History and Interpretation in John 10." In Beutler and Fortna, *Shepherd Discourse*, 53–74. Cambridge: Cambridge University Press, 1991.

Pfister, Friedrich. "Herakles und Christus." *Archiv für Religionswissenschaft* 34 (1937) 42–60.

Porter, Stanley E. "Why Hasn't Reader-Response Criticism Caught on in New Testament Studies?" *Journal of Literature and Theology* 4 (1990) 278–92.

Pritchard, J. B. ed. *Ancient Near Eastern Texts*. Princeton: Princeton University Press, 1955.

Quasten, Johannes. "Der Gute Hirte in frühchristlicher Totenliturgie und Grabeskunst." Chap. 10 in *Miscellanea Giovanni Mercati*, 373–406. Vol. 1, Studi e Testi, 121. Citta del Vaticano: Biblioteca Apostolica Vaticana, 1946.

———. "The Parable of the Good Shepherd: Jn.10:1–21." *CBQ* 10 (1948) 1–12, 151–69.

Reicke, Bo. *The Epistles of James, Peter and Jude*. The Anchor Bible 37. New York: Doubleday, 1964.

Reinhartz, Adele. "From Narrative to History: The Resurrection of Martha and Mary." In *Women Like This: New Perspectives on Jewish Women in the Greco-Roman World*, ed. Amy-Jill Levine, 161–84. SBLEJL 1. Atlanta: Scholars Press, 1991.

————. "Great Expectations; A Reader-Oriented Approach to Johannine Christology and Eschatology." *Journal of Literature and Theology* 3 (1989) 61–76.

————. "Jesus as Prophet: Predictive Prolepses in the Fourth Gospel." *JSNT* 36 (1989) 3–16.

————. "The New Testament and Anti-Judaism: A Literary-Critical Approach." *JES* 25 (1988) 524–37.

————. "The Shepherd and the Sheep: John 10:1–5 Reconsidered." *Proceedings of the Eastern Great Lakes Biblical Society* 9 (1989) 161–77.

Riesenfeld, Harald. "Zu den johanneischen *hina*-Sätzen." *ST* 19 (1965) 213–20.

Rihbany, A. M. *The Syrian Christ.* 2d. ed. London: Andrew Melrose, 1920.

Robinson, J.A.T. "The Parable of John 10:1–5." *ZNW* 46 (1955) 233–40.

Russell, J. B. *Satan: The Early Christian Tradition.* Ithaca: Cornell University Press, 1981.

Sabbe, M. "John 10 and its Relationship to the Synoptic Gospels." In Beutler and Fortna, *Shepherd Discourse*, 75–93.

Sanders, J. A. *The Dead Sea Psalms Scroll.* Ithaca: Cornell University Press, 1967.

Sandmel, Samuel. *Anti-Semitism in the New Testament?* Philadelphia: Fortress, 1978.

Schnackenburg, Rudolf. "Die Messiasfrage im Johannesevangelium." In *Neutestamentliche Aufsätze: Festschrift für Josef Schmid*, ed. Josef Binzler, 240–64. Regensburg: Pustet, 1963.

Schneider, Carl. "Herakles der Todüberwinder." *Wissenschaftliche Zeitschrift der Karl-Marx Universität* 7 (1958) 661–66.

————. *Geistesgeschichte des Antiken Christentums.* Bd. 1. Munich: C.H. Beck'sche Verlagsbuchhandlung, 1954.

Schoeps, H. J. *Jewish Christianity.* Philadelphia: Fortress, 1969.

Schwartz, E. "Osterbetrachtungen." *ZNW* 7 (1906) 5.

Scott, Bernard Brandon. *Hear Then the Parable: A Commentary on the Parables of Jesus*. Minneapolis: Fortress, 1989.

Segovia, Fernando F. "The Journey(s) of the Word of God: A Reading of the Plot of the Fourth Gospel." In *The Fourth Gospel From a Literary Perspective*, ed. R. Alan Culpepper and Fernando F. Segovia. *Semeia* 53 (1991) 23–54.

Simonis, A. J. *Die Hirtenrede im Johannes-Evangelium*. Rom: Päpstliches Bibelsinstitut, 1967.

Smith, Dwight Moody, Jr. *The Composition and Order of the Fourth Gospel*. New Haven: Yale University Press, 1965.

Staley, Jeffrey Lloyd. *The Print's First Kiss: A Rhetorical Investigation of the Implied Reader in the Fourth Gospel*. SBLDS 82. Atlanta: Scholars Press, 1988.

Stephanus, Henrico, ed. *Thesaurus Graecae Linguae*. 8 vols. Paris: Ambrosius Firmin Didot, 1831–56.

Sternberg, Meir. *The Poetics of Biblical Narrative*. Bloomington: Indiana University Press, 1987.

Tanzer, Sarah J. "Salvation is for the Jews: Secret Christian Jews in the Gospel of John." In *The Future of Early Christianity: Essays in Honor of Helmut Koester*, ed. Birger Pearson, 285–300. Minneapolis: Fortress, 1991.

Thaniel, George. "Themes of Death in Roman Religion and Poetry." Ph.D. diss., McMaster University, 1971.

Thomson, W. M. *The Land and the Book*. London: Nelson, 1891.

Tobin, T. H. "The Prologue of John and Hellenistic Jewish Speculation." *CBQ* 52 (1990) 252–69.

Tolbert, Mary Ann. *Perspectives on the Parables: An Approach to Multiple Interpretations*. Philadelphia: Fortress, 1979.

———. *Sowing the Gospel: Mark's World in Literary-Historical Perspective*. Minneapolis: Fortress, 1989.

Turner, John D. "The History of Religions Background of John 10." In Beutler and Fortna, *Shepherd Discourse*, 33–52.

Van der Watt, J. G. "A New Look at John 5:25–29 in the Light of the Use of the Term 'Eternal Life' in the Gospel according to John." *Neot* 19 (1985) 71–86.

———. "The Use of αἰώνιος in the Concept ζωὴ αἰώνιος in John's Gospel." *NovT* 31 (1989) 217–28.

Van Dijk, S. J. P. "The Bible in Liturgical Use." In *The Cambridge History of the Bible*. Vol. 2, ed. G. W. H. Lampe, 220–52. Cambridge: Cambridge University Press, 1969.

Via, Dan Otto, Jr. *The Parables: Their Literary and Existential Dimension.* Philadelphia: Fortress, 1967.

Von Campenhausen, Hans, ed. *Die Religion in Geschichte und Gegenwart.* 7 vols. Tübingen: J. C. B. Mohr, 1959.

Wenz, Helmut. "Sehen und Glauben bei Johannes." *TZ* 17 (1961) 17–25.

Woll, D. Bruce. *Johannine Christianity in Conflict.* SBLDS 60. Chico, Calif.: Scholars Press, 1981.

Zandee, J. *Death as an Enemy According to Ancient Egyptian Conceptions.* Leiden: Brill, 1960.

Index of Biblical Citations

INDEX OF AUTHORS

INDEX OF SUBJECTS